The Twelve Steps

**The Church's Challenge
and Opportunity**

MINISTRY SOLUTIONS

THE

The Church's Challenge and Opportunity

By Charles T. Knippel

SAINT LOUIS

For my wife, Donna
and our children, Arthur, David, Martin, Charles
and Anne Marie

Copyright © 1994 Concordia Publishing House
3558 S. Jefferson Avenue, St. Louis, MO 63118-3968
Manufactured in the United States of America

Library of Congress Cataloging-in-Publication Data

Knippel, Charles T., 1927–
    The twelve steps: the church's challenge and opportunity/Charles T. Knippel.
       p.   cm.
    Includes bibliographical references
    ISBN 0-570-04653-X
    1. Twelve-step programs—Religious aspects—Christiantiy. 2. Spiritual life—
Christianity. I. Title.
    BV4501.2.K55   1994
    261.8' 3229186—dc20
                                                   94-8327

1 2 3 4 5 6 7 8 9 10   03 02 01 00 99 98 97 96 95 94

Contents

Preface

I have written this book for professional church workers and all who are interested in assessing and using the Twelve Steps from a biblical perspective. This book is born out of my interests and experiences as a parish pastor, a pastor working in the area of chemical dependency with the Lutheran Ministries Association of Metropolitan St. Louis, and a teacher of "Pastoral Theology" and "Pastoral Care for Chemical Dependents and Their Families" at Concordia Seminary in St. Louis, Missouri. In turn, it results in many ways from research in the late 1980s for my doctoral dissertation at St. Louis University: "Samuel M. Shoemaker's Theological Influence on William G. Wilson's Twelve Step Spiritual Program of Recovery."

The preparation of this book has aided me greatly in formulating my personal biblical and pastoral concerns and responses with regard to the Twelve Step Program. I hope it will help you to discover for your own well-being and for the care of others what challenges and opportunities the steps provide for the church.

As this book shows, I deeply respect the Twelve Steps. Yet my commitment in preparing this assessment has been to look critically at the steps and their implications from the perspective of biblical and evangelical Christianity.

After 40 years of pastoral ministry, I cannot possibly identify everyone I should thank for their contributions to the thoughts expressed in this work. There have been so many helpful people in my life. Yet, I certainly thank my family of origin; my wife and children; my teachers; parishioners in Illinois, Oklahoma, and Missouri; colleagues; students; and the many people I know and value who practice the Twelve Step Spiritual Program of Recovery. I, of course, owe a great debt of gratitude to my wife, Donna Marie, for her love and support.

I am deeply grateful for the editing work that shaped this book for publication. I extend heartfelt thanks to the Reverend David V. Koch for his interest, encouragement, and advice.

I pray that God, who enabled me to write this book, will be pleased to use it in the interest of His kingdom coming among us and others. I give Him heartfelt thanks and praise!

Acknowledgments

Quotation from *Concerned Intervention* by John and Pat O'Neill. Copyright ©1993 by Harbinger Publications, Inc. Reprinted by permission. ❖ Material from The Twelve Steps, portions from *Alcoholics Anonymous, Alcoholics Anonymous Comes of Age,* and *'Pass It On': The Story of Bill Wilson* and *How the A. A. Message Reached the World* are reprinted with permission of Alcoholics Anonymous World Services, Inc. Permission to reprint this material does not mean that AA has reviewed or approved the contents of this publication, nor that AA agrees with the views expressed herein. ❖ Quotations from *12 Steps to Destruction* used with permission from Martin and Deidre Bobgan, ©1991 EastGate Publishers, 4137 Primavera Rd., Santa Barbara, CA 93110. ❖ Quotation from *Lois Remembers*, copyright ©1979 by Al-Anon Family Group Headquarters, Inc. Reprinted by permission of Al-Anon Family Group Headquarters, Inc. ❖ Quotations from *Not God: A History of Alcoholics Anonymous,* copyright 1979 by Hazeldon Founation, Center City, MN. Reprinted by permission. ❖ Quotations from The Papers of Samuel M. Shoemaker, Archives of the Episcopal Church. Used by permission. ❖ SELECTED FROM PAGE 59 from HOW TO BECOME A CHRISTIAN by SAMUEL M. SHOEMAKER. Copyright 1953 by Harper & Brothers. Copyright Renewed. Reprinted by permission of HarperCollins Publisher, Inc. ❖ Quotation from Samuel M. Shoemaker, *Christ and This Crisis* (New York: Fleming H. Revell Co., 1943). Used by permission. ❖ SELECTED FROM PAGE 40 from WITH THE HOLY SPIRIT AND WITH FIRE by SAMUEL M. SHOEMAKER. Copyright ©1960 by Samuel M. Shoemaker. Copyright Renewed 1988 by Helen Shoemaker. Reprinted by permission of HarperCollins Publishers, Inc. ❖ Quotation reprinted by permission from THE ROAD TO RECOVERY by Dennis Morreim, copyright ©1990 Augsburg Fortress. ❖ Quotation from *The Twelve Steps in the Bible* by Michele S. Matto. Copyright ©1991 Paulist Press. Reprinted by permission. ❖ SELECTED FROM PAGE XIII from A HUNGER FOR HEALING by J. KEITH MILLER. Copyright ©1991 by John Keith Miller. Reprinted by permission of HarperCollins Publishers, Inc. ❖ Quotations reprinted from THE BOOK OF CONCORD by T. G. Tappert, copyright ©1959 Fortress Press. Used by permission of Augsburg Fortress. ❖ Quotation from *A Short Exposition of Dr. Martin Luther's Small Catechism ... WITH ADDITIONAL NOTES* by Edward W. A. Koehler reprinted by permission by Concordia Theological Seminary Press, Ft. Wayne, IN. ❖ Quotation reprinted from THEOLOGY OF THE LUTHERAN CONFESSIONS by Edmund Schlink, copyright ©1961 Fortress Press. Used by permission of Augsburg Fortress. ❖ Quotation reprinted from LUTHERS'S WORKS, Volume 45, edited by Helmut T. Lehman, copyright ©1962 Fortress Press. Used by permission of Augsburg Fortress. ❖ Quotation reprinted from THE ETHICS OF MARTIN LUTHER by Paul Althaus; translated by Robert C. Schultz, copyright ©1972 Fortress Press. Used by permission of Augsburg Fortress. ❖ Quotation reprinted from The Ethics of Martin Luther by Paul Althaus; translated by Robert C. Schultz, copyright ©1972 Fortress Press. Used by permission of Augsburg Fortress. ❖ SELECTED FROM PAGE 72 from REVIVE THY CHURCH BEGINNING WITH ME by SAMUEL M. SHOEMAKER. Copyright 1948 by Samuel Moor Shoemaker. Copyright Renewed 1976 by Helen Smith Shoemaker. Reprinted by permission of HarperCollins Publishers, Inc.

Introduction

Twentieth-Century Phenomenon

Millions of people throughout the world are recovering from various addictive and coaddictive lifestyles by practicing principles known as the Twelve Steps. Twelve Step practitioners represent many religious faiths and no religious faith. You may be one of them. You may have relatives, friends, or neighbors who belong to Twelve Step groups. Or you, or persons you know, may be considering trying the Twelve Step program.

In their book *Concerned Intervention*, John and Pat O'Neill highlight the importance of the Twelve Steps of Alcoholics Anonymous, especially for chemically dependent persons. The O'Neills speak enthusiastically about the success of the Twelve Step Program:

> Millions of C.D. [chemically dependent] people have found a practical pathway to spirituality in the Twelve Steps of Alcoholics Anonymous. A.A. is the unchallenged fountainhead from which has flowed our stubborn national acceptance of alcoholism as a treatable disease. Scott Peck, author of the immensely popular *The Road Less Traveled*, ranks A.A. among the three most important innovations of this century along with television and the jet airplane. And deservedly so. He does this because the entire concept of self-help began with A.A. A.A. has saved more individual alcoholic lives and families than everything else ever tried combined. The famous Twelve Steps upon which the program is based has been adapted successfully for just about every compulsive behavior known.[1]

Over fifty years ago William G. Wilson (1895-1971), one of the principal cofounders of Alcoholics Anonymous (A.A.), formulated the Twelve Steps. Anonymously he was known as Bill

9

W., but he disclosed his full identity. In putting the steps into their final shape, Bill had the assistance of other recovering alcoholics, especially Dr. Robert Holbrook Smith (Dr. Bob), the other chief cofounder of A.A. Their contributions grew out of their personal recovery experiences.

Bill W. and his colleagues first published the Twelve Steps in 1939 in the book *Alcoholics Anonymous*, also known as the "Big Book." These steps have remained unchanged in both the second and third editions of the "Big Book."

Groups in addition to Alcoholics Anonymous (A.A.) that use the Twelve Steps include Al-Anon, Narcotics Anonymous, Smokers Anonymous, Sexaholics Anonymous, Gamblers Anonymous, and Overeaters Anonymous. Estimates suggest that Alcoholics Anonymous alone has a worldwide membership of more than 1.5 million people.

The Twelve Steps

In a first draft of the steps Wilson spoke of God without qualification. However, in order to satisfy recovering alcoholics who claimed to be atheists or agnostics and to make the recovery program available to people of all faiths or no faith at all, Bill reworked the steps to refer to God as "Higher Power" and to "God *as we understood Him*."

In *Alcoholics Anonymous* Bill W. stated the Twelve Step Program as follows:

Remember that we deal with alcohol—cunning, baffling, powerful! Without help it is too much for us. But there is One who has all power—that One is God. May you find Him now!

Half measures availed us nothing. We stood at the turning point. We asked His protection and care with complete abandon.

Here are the steps we took, which are suggested as a Program of Recovery.

1. We admitted we were powerless over alcohol, that our lives had become unmanageable.

2. Came to believe that a Power greater than ourselves could restore us to sanity.
3. Made a decision to turn our will and our lives over to the care of God *as we understood Him.*
4. Made a searching and fearless moral inventory of ourselves.
5. Admitted to God, to ourselves, and to another human being the exact nature of our wrongs.
6. Were entirely ready to have God remove all these defects of character.
7. Humbly asked Him to remove our shortcomings.
8. Made a list of all persons we had harmed, and became willing to make amends to them all.
9. Made direct amends to such people wherever possible, except when to do so would injure them or others.
10. Continued to take personal inventory and when we were wrong promptly admitted it.
11. Sought through prayer and meditation to improve our conscious contact with God *as we understood Him,* praying only for knowledge of His will for us and the power to carry that out.
12. Having had a spiritual awakening as the result of these steps, we tried to carry this message to alcoholics, and to practice these principles in all our affairs.[2]

Christians Disagree about the Twelve Steps

In recent years Christian authors have published a variety of books and articles about the Twelve Step Program because of its religious connotations. It is known as a *spiritual* program of recovery, and it refers the practitioner to the "Higher Power" and to "God *as we understood Him*" for help.

The Twelve Steps confront the Christian with questions that ask for biblical answers. How shall we regard a recovery program that directs people seeking spiritual help to a nonspecific Higher Power and to God *as we understood Him?*

How shall we respond to principles of recovery that do not explicitly recognize Jesus as Savior and Lord? Can the Bible enable us to understand how the Twelve Steps can work in people's lives even though these steps are not Christ-centered? Can Christians use the Twelve Steps to deal with certain problems of life in God-pleasing ways?

Christian writers disagree about the value of the Twelve Step Spiritual Program of Recovery. Some authors view the Twelve Steps as totally unacceptable for Christians and non-Christians alike. Martin and Deidre Bobgan, for example, characterize them as *12 Steps to Destruction.* In *Alcoholics Anonymous Unmasked: Deception and Deliverance* Cathy Burns, like the Bobgans, expresses strong opposition to the Twelve Steps.[3]

Other Christian writers take a different approach. They look for ways to interpret the steps biblically and then recommend them for Christian use. One such author has published an article about "The Hidden Gospel of the 12 Steps." Others have written books entitled *The Twelve Steps for Christians; The Twelve Steps in the Bible; A Hunger for Healing: The Twelve Steps as a Classic Model for Christian Spiritual Growth*; and *The Road to Recovery: Bridges Between the Bible and the Twelve Steps.*[4]

Of greater interest is the fact that both the authors who oppose and those who approve of the Twelve Steps tend not to use biblical resources to make a critical Christian assessment of the steps. This is unfortunate, because the steps challenge the church to provide an adequate and accurate Bible-based appraisal. To be more specific, the steps challenge the church to base its appraisal on what the Bible says God, in His Law, expects of people He has created and what God, through His Good News in Jesus Christ, freely gives us to make us His own and to renew our lives.

Challenge and Opportunity

The Twelve Steps pose a huge challenge for the church, but they also offer the church extraordinary opportunity. As we shall see, the steps provide the church an opportunity to enhance the shape and scope of its ministry among people both inside and outside the church.

This book explores both the challenge and opportunity the Twelve Steps set before the church. The very nature of this undertaking implies that it is neither appropriate summarily to reject the Twelve Steps nor accurate to look for the Gospel and the fullness of God's blessings where they cannot be found. Furthermore, it indicates that an interpretation of the program for Christian use needs to be scripturally faithful and forthright in identifying both right and wrong religious concepts in the Twelve Step Program and biblically sound in crafting God-pleasing conclusions and suggestions.

Our Approach

Specific Bible teachings present themselves as particularly relevant to our undertaking: what people can know about God naturally, without revelation; the idea of civil righteousness, that is, what people who are not yet Christians can do in fulfilling outwardly God's Law; the role of human will in performing such outward good actions for the well-being of others; and God's rule in the secular sphere of life as compared with His spiritual rule.

We shall pursue our goals in specific ways, beginning with the origin and meaning of the Twelve Steps. Only then will we be ready to give serious attention to the challenge and opportunity the steps place before the church. As already expressed, we will use the Bible as the primary source for shaping evaluations and recommendations to assist one another in dealing with the Twelve Steps in ways God Himself directs.

---

1. John and Pat O'Neill, *Concerned Intervention* (Oakland CA: New Harbinger Publications, Inc., 1993), 172–73.

2. [William G. Wilson et al.], *Alcoholics Anonymous,* rev. 2d ed. (New York: Alcoholics Anonymous Publishing, Inc., 1955), 59–60.

3. Martin and Deidre Bobgan, *12 Steps to Destruction* (Santa Barbara: EastGate Publishers, 1991); Cathy Burns, *Alcoholics Anonymous Unmasked: Deception and Deliverance* (Shippenburg, PA: Companion Press, 1991).

4. Tim Stafford, "The Hidden Gospel of the 12 Steps," *Christianity Today* (July 22, 1991); *The Twelve Steps for Christians* (San Diego: Recovery Publications, 1988); Michele S. Matto, *The 12 Steps in the Bible* (New York: Paulist Press, 1991); L. Keith Miller, *A Hunger for Healing: The Twelve Steps as a Classic Model for Christian Spiritual Growth* (San Francisco: Harper, 1991); Dennis C. Morreim, *The Road to Recovery: Bridges between the Bible and the Twelve Steps* (Minneapolis: Augsburg, 1990).

Part 1

The Twelve Steps—Their Origin and Meaning

Chapter 1

A Sketch of Bill W.'s Life

Early Years

William Griffith Wilson, Bill W. in Alcoholics Anonymous circles, principal author of the Twelve Steps, was born on November 26, 1895, in East Dorset in the midst of Vermont's marble quarry country on the western slopes of the Green Mountains. He entered the world in the Wilson House, a village inn run by his father's widowed mother, the older of two children born to Gilman Barrows and Emily Griffith Wilson.

William Wilson lived and went to school in East Dorset until, in 1903, his father, Gilman Wilson, took a job as the manager of the Rutland-Florence quarry, moving his family 25 miles away. In 1905 Gilman Wilson deserted his family, and the next year Bill's mother, Emily, moved him and his sister, Dorothy, back to East Dorset where they lived with Gardner Fayette and Ella Griffith, their maternal grandparents. After divorcing Gilman Wilson, Bill's mother left him and his sister with her parents and went to Boston to study to become an osteopathic physician.

In the fall of 1909 William Wilson began his secondary studies at Burr and Burton Seminary, a high school in Manchester, Vermont. At Burr and Burton Seminary Bill met Edwin (Ebby) Thatcher, later known as Ebby T., who would play a major role in Bill's recovery from alcoholism.

While enrolled at Burr and Burton Seminary, Bill fell in love with a schoolmate, Bertha Bamford, who died following tumor surgery during Bill's senior year. After her death Bill became deeply depressed, and as a result, his academic performance deteriorated to the extent that he failed to graduate with his class. He then went to live with his mother near Boston and there completed studies that qualified him for college.

First Drink and Marriage

In the summer of 1913 Bill met Lois Burnham, the oldest daughter of a New York physician, whom he married five years later. In the fall of 1914, at age nineteen, Bill entered Norwich University, a military college in Northfield, Vermont. Called up by the military when the United States entered World War I in 1917, Bill did not graduate from Norwich. Rather, he entered the officers training camps at Plattsburg, New York, and Fort Monroe, Virginia. Commissioned a Second Lieutenant in the Army Artillery, he was assigned to Fort Rodman, just outside New Bedford, Massachusetts. While at Fort Rodman, Bill, at age 22, took his first drink, became intoxicated, and began 17 years of alcoholic drinking. Reflecting on this years later, Bill's wife, Lois, offered this reason for Bill's abstinence from alcoholic beverages prior to his army experience. She commented:

> Bill had been warned since childhood not to touch alcohol. His mother had divorced his father largely because of drink, he thought. His paternal grandfather had also had bad drinking episodes, but through some kind of transforming experience had stopped drinking completely. If Bill once began, he had been warned, he, too, might get into trouble. He believed this and decided not to drink. Later I marveled that this had been enough reason for a man like Bill, whose independent spirit always led him into experimenting.[1]

On January 24, 1918, William Wilson and Lois Burnham were married in Brooklyn, New York, in the Swedenborgian Church, the church in which Lois was raised. Six months later, on July 18, 1918, Bill went overseas. He sailed from Boston to Europe where he was first stationed outside Winchester, England, and then in France. When the war ended on November 11, 1918, Wilson had seen no active combat. Discharged from the Army in May of 1919, he and Lois settled in Brooklyn, New York.

Work on Wall Street

Right after the war Bill had a number of jobs in New York City. For a time he worked as a clerk in the insurance department of the New York Central Railroad and as an investigator in fraud and embezzlement for the United States Fidelity and Guaranty Company. He also enrolled in night classes at the Brooklyn Law School. There he completed the requirements for a diploma at the law school but, because of his drinking, he failed to appear at the right time to receive it.

During the 1920s and early 1930s Bill Wilson had a variety of employment positions related to the stock market business, primarily on Wall Street. In the early 1930s he also had frequent periods of unemployment. His drinking and attendant behavior interfered increasingly with his personal and business life.

At the time of the 1929 Stock Market Crash, Bill and Lois were $60,000 in debt. A short time later they went to live in the Burnham home at 182 Clinton Street in Brooklyn. Lois' mother died on Christmas Day in 1930, and Bill and Lois lived with Dr. Burnham on Clinton Street until the physician remarried in early 1933 and moved from the family home, leaving Bill and Lois as the only residents.

Hospitalizations and Ebby's Visits

On four separate occasions during 1933 and 1934 Bill Wilson entered the Charles B. Towns Hospital for alcoholism treatment. There Dr. William Duncan Silkworth taught Bill that alcoholism is an illness—a combination of a physical allergy and a mental obsession—characterized by loss of control over the use of alcohol.

Between Towns Hospital treatment periods Bill had visits from his old friend, Ebby T., who like Bill had become an alcoholic drinker. In November 1934 Ebby Thatcher first visited Bill on Clinton Street. Ebby was sober and told Bill he had "sobered up" because he had "gotten religion." Even though Bill was not initially attracted to Ebby's talk about religion, he nevertheless listened to Ebby tell his story about how old drinking friends, Shep, Cebra, and Rowland, had introduced him to the Oxford Group. Ebby reported that as a result of their influence he had come into contact with Calvary Episcopal Mission on 23rd Street in New York City where Oxford Group principles were taught and practiced.

Bill provided this personal account of Ebby's conversation with him in an address in St. Louis on the occasion of the 20th anniversary of Alcoholics Anonymous:

> What a crusher that was—Ebby and religion! Maybe his alcoholic insanity had become religious insanity. It was an awful letdown. I had been educated at a wonderful engineering college where somehow I gathered the impression that man was God. But I had to be polite, so I said, "What brand of religion have you got, Ebby?" "Oh," he said, "I don't think it has got any special brand name. I just fell in with a group of people, the Oxford Groups. I don't go along with all their teachings by any means. But those folks have given me some wonderful ideas. I learned that I had to admit I was licked; I learned that I ought to take stock of myself and confess my defects to another person in confidence; I learned that I needed to make restitution for the harm I had done others. I was told that I ought to practice the kind of giving that has no price tag on it, the giving of yourself to somebody. "Now," he added, "I know you are going to gag on this, but they taught me that I should try to pray to whatever God I thought there was for the power to carry out these simple precepts. And if I did not believe there was any God, then I had better try the experiment of praying to whatever God there *might* be. And you know, Bill, it's a queer thing, but even before I had done all this, just as soon as I decided that I would try with an open mind, it seemed to me that my drinking problem was lifted right out of me. It wasn't like the water wagon business at all. This time I felt completely released of the desire, and I have not had a drink for months."[2]

Ebby's visit brought to mind Bill's experience at Winchester Cathedral when he had been stationed as a soldier in England. There Bill had a religious experience which he called a "tremendous sense of presence." He later commented, "For a brief moment, I had needed and wanted God. There had been a humble willingness to have Him with me and He came."[3]

Religious Beliefs

For the most part, Bill Wilson had little place for God in his life and certainly no place for a personal God. Recounting his story in *Alcoholics Anonymous*, Bill told about his religious beliefs at the time of Ebby's confrontation. He recalled his childhood attendance at Sunday church services with a rather skeptical grandfather. Then he wrote a number of telling paragraphs to describe his own current convictions:

I had always believed in a power greater than myself. I had often pondered these things. I was not an atheist. Few people really are, for that means blind faith in the strange proposition that this universe originated in a cipher and aimlessly rushes nowhere . . . I simply had to believe in a Spirit of the Universe, who knew neither time nor limitation. But that was as far as I had gone.

With ministers, and the world's religions, I parted right there. When they talked of a God personal to me, who was love, superhuman strength and direction, I became irritated and my mind snapped shut against such a theory.

To Christ I conceded the certainty of a great man, not too closely followed by those who claimed Him. His moral teaching most excellent. For myself, I had adopted those parts which seemed convenient and not too difficult; the rest I disregarded.[4]

In *Not-God: A History of Alcoholics Anonymous* Ernest Kurtz observes that little is known of Wilson's early exposure to religion, probably because there is little to know. Kurtz calls Bill's maternal grandfather "an Ingersoll-inclined transcendentalist," and notes that "young Bill Wilson had 'left the church' at about age twelve on 'a matter of principle.' " He records that this principle concerned a required temperance pledge. Even at Burr and Burton Seminary, where chapel was the custom, Bill revealed that he "had no 'religion' beyond an adolescent romanticism easily congruent with both his grandfather's Vermont vagueness and his friend Mark Whalon's adoring admiration of the power of the human mind."[5]

With regard to the role of religion in Bill W.'s life, biographer Robert Thomsen makes the interesting observation that before his final hospitalizations Bill read Mary Baker Eddy's *Science and Health*.[6]

In spite of his avowed disbelief in a personal God and his animosity toward organized religion, after a second visit from Ebby, accompanied by Shep C., Bill decided to attend an Oxford Group meeting at the Calvary Rescue Mission operated by Calvary Episcopal Church, Dr. Samuel M. Shoemaker, rector. He could not forget Ebby's talk about how God had helped him, nor could he deny that something had happened: Ebby was sober. He was driven to investigate the Oxford Group and its teachings.

Even though Bill visited Calvary Mission and attended an evening service at which he reportedly gave his life to God while he was intoxicated, his visit did not bring an immediate end to his drinking. He continued to drink for two or three more days until he admitted himself on December 11, 1934, for another stay at Town's Hospital.

Spiritual Awakening

During Bill's hospitalization Ebby T. visited him again to offer encouragement. Personally, Bill could see nothing ahead but death or insanity. He was deeply depressed. But in the very midst of his feelings of helplessness and desperation Bill had an experience which he came to call his spiritual awakening. The A.A. book *'Pass It On': The Story of Bill Wilson and How the Message of A.A. Reached the World* includes Bill's own telling recounting of his experience:

Now, he and Lois were waiting for the end. Now, there was nothing ahead but death or madness. This was the finish, the jumping off place. "The terrifying darkness had become complete," Bill said. "In agony of spirit, I again thought of the cancer of alcoholism which had now consumed me in mind and spirit and soon the body." The abyss gaped before him.

In his helplessness and desperation, Bill cried out, "I'll do anything, anything at all!" He had reached a point of total, utter, deflation—a state of complete, absolute surrender. With neither faith nor hope, he cried, "If there be a God, let Him show Himself!"

What happened next was electric. "Suddenly, my room blazed beyond description. Every joy I had known was pale by comparison. The light, the ecstasy—I was conscious of nothing else for a time.

"Then, seen in the mind's eye, there was a mountain. I stood upon its summit, where a great wind blew. A wind, not of air, but of spirit. In great, clean strength, it blew right through me. Then came the blazing thought 'You are a free man.' I know not at all how long I remained in this state, but finally the light and the ecstasy subsided. I again saw the wall of my room. As I became more quiet, a great peace stole over me, and this was accompanied by a sensation difficult to describe. I became acutely conscious of a Presence which seemed like a veritable sea of living spirit. I lay on the shores of a new world. 'This,' I thought, 'must be the great reality. The God of the preachers.'

"Savoring my new world, I remained in this state for a long time. I seemed to be possessed by the absolute, and the curious conviction deepened that no matter how wrong things seemed to be, there could be no question of the ultimate rightness of God's universe. For the first time, I felt that I really belonged. I knew that I was loved and could love in return. I thanked my God, who had given me a glimpse of His absolute self. Even though a pilgrim upon an uncertain highway, I need be concerned no more, for I had glimpsed the great beyond."[7]

Bill had just begun his 40th year when this experience radically changed his life. From that time on he did not doubt the existence of a personal and loving God. He never took another alcoholic drink.

Soon after his spiritual experience, while still hospitalized, Bill read William James' *Varieties of Religious Experience.* One of his friends, most likely Ebby T., brought him a copy of the book, saying that it was recommended by the Oxford Group. In James' book Bill read case histories of experiences like his own and noted three common denominators of such experiences: personal calamity, utter desperation, and an appeal to a Higher Power. He also noted that such experiences might result in either sudden or gradual transformations. The author of '*Pass It On*' observes that James' "insights became important to Bill in his thinking about the plight of the alcoholic and his need for spiritual help."[8] They also ratified Bill's own experience.

Not long after his spiritual awakening Bill began thinking about a movement of recovered alcoholic persons who would help other alcoholics. "At this point," he later recalled, "my excitement became boundless. A chain reaction could be set in motion, forming an ever-growing fellowship of alcoholics, whose mission it would be to visit the caves of still other sufferers and set them free."[9]

After Bill's release from Towns Hospital, he and his wife, Lois, began to attend Oxford Group meetings at Calvary Episcopal Church. At the same time, he and Ebby began to work with problem drinkers at Calvary Mission and Towns Hospital. Bill also met with a small group of former problem drinkers who attended Oxford Group meetings and afterwards gathered for their own meeting at a neighborhood cafeteria. Bill and Lois frequently opened their Clinton Street home as a lodging place for men struggling with their alcoholism.

Dr. Bob and A.A.'s Birth

In May of 1935 Bill made a business trip to Akron, Ohio, in the interest of the National Rubber Machinery Company. His business affairs did not go well, and Bill was tempted to drink. Instead, he picked the name of Episcopal priest, Walter F. Tunks, from the Mayflower Hotel church directory and telephoned him in an attempt to locate an alcoholic with whom he might work and thus find some personal help in his difficult moment. Through the referrals of Father Tunks, Bill came into contact with Henrietta Seiberling, a nonalcoholic member of the Akron Oxford Group. Henrietta, in turn, put Bill in touch with Dr. Robert Holbrook Smith, an Akron surgeon and Oxford Group member, struggling with his own serious drinking problem.

Within a matter of weeks Dr. Bob sobered up as a result of his relationship with Bill. On June 10, 1935, Dr. Bob took his last drink, and Alcoholics Anonymous, yet to be so named, was born in Akron, Ohio. Bill Wilson stayed in the Smith home in Akron for a number of months. During that time two other problem drinkers were added to the then nameless fellowship of now-sober alcoholics.

In late August of 1935 Bill returned to New York City. He and Lois resumed attending the Oxford Group meetings at Dr. Shoemaker's church and participated in several Oxford Group houseparties. In addition, in the fall of 1935 Bill and Lois began to hold weekly meetings for alcoholics on Tuesday evenings in their home on Clinton Street. The number of sober alcoholics increased.

By 1937 Bill W. and Dr. Bob could count 40 cases of recovered alcoholics in Ohio and New York. To give the new movement the legal structure of a tax-exempt charitable trust, Bill, other recovering alcoholics, and nonalcoholic friends established the Alcoholic Foundation with a board of trustees on August 11, 1938. Later the new fellowship called this foundation the General Service Board of Alcoholics Anonymous.

The Big Book

Because both Bill W. and Dr. Bob wanted to reach out beyond their geographic regions with the message of recovery, in 1937 they began to discuss writing a book about their recovery experiences. Even though Bill conferred with Dr. Bob and other sober alcoholics, he was the author of at least 10, maybe all 11, of the opening chapters of the envisioned book. Sixteen of the life stories came from recovering persons in Akron, and 12 from New York. Ultimately named *Alcoholics Anonymous,* the book appeared in its first edition in April, 1939, and included the statement of Wilson's Twelve Steps. The title of the book quickly became the name of the fellowship of sober alcoholics.

Father Dowling

After the publication of *Alcoholics Anonymous,* Bill W. continued to work full-time for the success of Alcoholics Anonymous in bringing recovery to alcoholic persons. During the winter of 1940 he met a man who became a valued friend and spiritual adviser to him for the next 20 years. He was Father Edward Dowling, a Jesuit priest from St. Louis, Missouri. The two men met when Dowling paid a personal visit to Bill W. in New York City after the priest had become acquainted with the Twelve Steps and noted the similarity of their content to the spiritual exercises of St. Ignatius Loyola. Concerning Father Dowling's visit and the ensuing relationship, the author of *'Pass It On'* reveals the following:

> That evening, Father Ed began sharing with Bill an understanding of the spiritual life that then and ever after seemed to speak to Bill's condition. Bill, author of the Fifth Step, would later characterize that evening as the night he took his Fifth Step, and also as a "second conversion experience." He unburdened himself of his commissions and omissions, all of which had lain heavily on his mind, and of which he had found, until then, no way to speak. This extraordinary communication, this openness of sharing, was to be vital for Bill. Father Dowling's "spiritual sponsorship" would endure, grow, and be nourished during a correspondence and a deep friendship that would last for the next two decades. The subjects of this interchange, although interspersed with "business" matters

of the Fellowship—Father Ed was one of its staunchest supporters, responsible for founding A.A. in St. Louis—were almost always questions Bill continued to ask throughout his life, about faith and no faith, about the church and its role in human affairs.[10]

Separation from OG

Nineteen thirty-seven turned out to be a particularly significant year in the history of A.A. In that year Bill W. and the New York fellowship of sober alcoholics separated from the Oxford Group and thus from a close association with the Rev. Samuel Shoemaker of Calvary Episcopal Church. Not until the early 1940s did Bill and Sam re-establish a close friendship.

Bill and Lois moved into their own home in 1941. For the first time in 23 years of married life they had a place of their own. Located in Bedford Hills, New York, it came to be called Stepping Stones. Bill had an office in New York City as well as a study at home. He traveled to speak to A.A. groups and Lois often accompanied him.

Religion and Psychic Experimentation

In his later years Bill Wilson continued to be interested in a wide range of religious experience, though he never committed himself fully to any given expression. In the 1940s and 1950s Bill experimented with psychic phenomena. In the latter part of the 1940s, he took instruction in the Roman Catholic faith from Monsignor, later Bishop, Fulton J. Sheen. Bill did not, however, become a member of the Roman Catholic Church. He was unable to accept some of its teachings, and furthermore he believed that as a cofounder of A.A. he should not associate himself with a particular religious denomination.

In a letter dated May 15, 1986, Lois Wilson, Bill's widow, wrote to the author that she believed Bill was a Christian and explained her understanding of that conviction. "As for your last question, Bill was a Christian, which to him meant being a proponent of Christian principles and a Christian way of life."[11] A rather comprehensive, and yet not altogether clear, statement of Bill Wilson's religious beliefs is found in a letter he wrote to Roman Catholic priest John C. Ford, S.J., on May 14, 1957. Bill summarized his religious beliefs as follows:

> Summing up, I can say that my experience caused me instantaneously to believe and know that God is my Father; that His grace is available to me; that life goes on beyond the grave; and that in His house there are many Mansions. These are the things I think I know. All the rest are in the nature of speculations which are subject to change on more evidence or better insight. I have tried very hard for Christianity as you understand it. But theologically speaking, I have never been able to go the whole way, notwithstanding my immense debt to Our Lord. Maybe I shall have to go on being a shopper at the theological pie-counter, though I hope not. The only theology of which I can be certain is the simple one just described.[12]

Last Years

During the 1940s Bill often suffered from deep depression. In 1944 he entered into psychiatric treatment with Dr. Harry Tiebout, a psychiatrist who had become a friend of A.A. That same year Alcoholics Anonymous moved its offices from Vesey Street to 415 Lexington Avenue in New York City. In June the *Grapevine* was first published as A.A.'s monthly periodical. In the April 1946 issue of the *Grapevine* Bill published the "Twelve Points to Assure Our Future," which were later called the Twelve Traditions. Bill saw these "Twelve Points" as the guidelines for the function and continuation of Alcoholics Anonymous as a unified fellowship.

In 1946 Bill W. earnestly began to work on his concept for a general service council to link local A.A. groups with the General Service Board and as a way of putting his proposed Twelve Traditions into operation. As a step in that direction, the First International Convention of Alcoholics Anonymous, held in Cleveland, Ohio, in 1950, adopted the Twelve Traditions as a corollary to the Twelve Steps and as necessary for the unity of the Fellowship of A.A. Later, at the 1955 Twentieth Anniversary Convention in St. Louis, Missouri, the General Service Conference received approval. Its purpose was to provide the means by which Alcoholics Anonymous would function through a democratic, representational, elected form of self-government.

After the First General Service Conference met in New York in April, 1951, Bill W. began work on his second book, *Twelve Steps and Twelve Traditions*. He produced an essay for each of the Twelve Steps and for each of the Twelve Traditions. Published in 1953, the book sets forth Bill W.'s second interpretation of the Twelve Steps.

In 1955 Bill published a second edition of *Alcoholics Anonymous*. In this edition, the first 11 chapters were left unchanged, as well as Bill W.'s, Dr. Bob's, and six other stories of changed-life experiences. Thirty new stories were added.

Bill Wilson's third book came off the press in 1957. Titled *Alcoholics Anonymous Comes of Age*, it gives his account of A.A.'s Twentieth Anniversary Convention in St. Louis, Missouri, when he turned over the leadership of Alcoholics Anonymous to the General Service Conference.

Between 1956 and 1959 Bill was involved in a second kind of experimentation. The first had been with psychic phenomena. In 1956 he entered into professionally directed experimentation with LSD, lysergic acid diethylamide. His purposes were to provide positive spiritual experiences for himself and others and to discover proof for survival after death. Speaking of his interest in proving life beyond death, Bill wrote:

> "Everything considered, I feel that full proof of survival would be one of the greatest events that could take place in the Western world today. It wouldn't necessarily make people good. But at least they could really know what God's plan is, as Christ so perfectly demonstrated at Easter time. Easter would become a fact; people could then live in a universe that would make sense."[13]

Encouraged by fellow A.A. members, Bill withdrew from the LSD experimentation in 1959 out of concern for the well-being of Alcoholics Anonymous and especially for those members who strongly objected to his participation. As the living person responsible for the origin of A.A., he did not want to endanger its present or future.

Even though his health was steadily declining, in his latter years Bill traveled and continued to work in the interest of Alcoholics Anonymous. On January 24, 1971, he died during his 76th year from the complications of emphysema. The day of his death was his and Lois' 53rd wedding anniversary. Bill was buried in the family plot in the East Dorset Cemetery in Vermont.

1. [Lois Wilson], *Lois Remembers* (New York: Al-Anon Family Group Headquarters, Inc., 1979), 22.

2. [William G. Wilson], *Alcoholics Anonymous Comes of Age* (New York: Alcoholics Anonymous Publishing, Inc., 1957), 58-59.

3. *'Pass It On': The Story of Bill Wilson and How the A.A. Message Reached the World* (New York: Alcoholics Anonymous World Services, 1984), 60.

4. [William G. Wilson et al.], *Alcoholics Anonymous*, rev. 2d ed. (New York: Alcoholics Anonymous Publishing, Inc., 1955), 10-11.

5. Ernest Kurtz, *Not-God: A History of Alcoholics Anonymous* (Center City, MN: Hazelden, 1979), 16.

6. Robert Thomsen, *Bill W.* (New York: Harper & Row, Publishers, 1975), 188.

7. *'Pass It On'*, 120-21.

8. Ibid., 124.

9. Ibid., 126.

10. Ibid., 242.

11. Lois B. Wilson to Charles T. Knippel, 15 May 1986.

12. William G. Wilson to John C. Ford, S.J., 14 May 1957, Shoemaker Papers, Record Group 101-30-26, Episcopal Church Archives, Austin, Texas.

13. *'Pass It On'*, 374.

Chapter 2

Bill W.'s Preparation of the Twelve Steps

The Big Book Begins

Bill W. had achieved three years of sobriety and Dr. Bob two and a half years, when in 1937, they began to talk about carrying their recovery program to alcoholics by publishing a book. Not too many months later, in March or April of 1938, Bill began work on the proposed book.

For the publication of the book, Hank P. formed a company named Works Publishing, Inc. In the small office he shared with Hank in Newark, New Jersey, Bill dictated the book to Ruth Hock, the office secretary. First, he completed his own personal story, followed by the chapter called "There Is a Solution."

As Bill continued to write notes and dictate the rough drafts, he sent copies of completed chapters to Dr. Bob for comment and discussed the material with the recovering alcoholics in New York. After crafting the chapters "More About Alcoholism" and "We Agnostics," Bill set himself to the task of writing the crucial chapter "How It Works." In this chapter he planned to set forth the steps of the spiritual recovery program, steps not yet formulated.

Drafting Twelve Steps

One evening in 1938 Bill set out to draft the steps for "How It Works." Lying on his bed at home on Clinton Street, with pencil in hand and a pad of yellow scratch paper on his knee, he asked for guidance and began to write. In about half an hour, Bill recalled, he expanded six principles he and his friends had learned from the Oxford Group into 12 principles or steps.

The first draft of the Twelve Steps has been lost, but *'Pass It On'* provides the following reconstruction:

1. We admitted we were powerless over alcohol—that our lives had become unmanageable.
2. Came to believe that God could restore us to sanity.
3. Made a decision to turn our wills and our lives over to the care and direction of God.
4. Made a searching and fearless moral inventory of ourselves.
5. Admitted to God, to ourselves, and to another human being the exact nature of our wrongs.
6. Were entirely willing that God remove all these defects of character.
7. Humbly on our knees asked Him to remove these shortcomings—holding nothing back.
8. Made a complete list of all persons we had harmed, and became willing to make amends to them all.
9. Made direct amends to such people wherever possible, except when to do so would injure them or others.
10. Continued to take personal inventory and when we were wrong promptly admitted it.
11. Sought through prayer and meditation to improve our contact with God, praying only for knowledge of His will for us and the power to carry that out.
12. Having had a spiritual experience as the result of this course of action, we tried to carry this message to others, especially alcoholics, and to practice these principles in all our affairs.[1]

Kurtz supplies Bill's preamble to the first draft of the Steps. Bill wrote:

"Rarely have we seen a person fail who has thoroughly followed our path." Bill's pencil began to fly over the paper, and his thoughts continued to flow as he wrote a paragraph beginning:

Half measures will avail you nothing. You stand at the turning point. Throw yourself under God's protection and care with complete abandon.

Now we think you can take it! Here are the steps we took [on] our program of recovery.[2]

Steps and Book Completed

As Bill W. wrote drafts of the book, he sought and received numerous reactions from the recovering alcoholics. Howard A. believed Bill had put too much talk about God in the Steps and objected to Bill's reference to getting down on one's knees to ask God's forgiveness for shortcomings. In all, Bill identified three groups of commentators. There were the conservatives, including Fritz M. and Paul K., who thought the book should be explicitly Christian. They favored using biblical terms and expressions. Liberals made up the largest group. They did not object to the use of the word "God" in the book, but they spoke against any particular theological-doctrinal positions and statements. They wanted a spiritual, but not a specifically religious, program. Then, there was the group Bill called the radical left wing. People like Henry and Jimmy represented the atheists and agnostics. They wanted the word "God" deleted from the book and preferred a psychological approach. Bill observed that the "liberals were the larger group, but they barely outnumbered the combined conservatives and radicals."[3]

A deliberate, carefully considered compromise emerged as the result of these disagreements. Initially Bill resisted the suggestion of compromise, but he finally accepted it because of the pluralistic thought among all involved. As a compromise he designed a restatement of the steps in which he described God as a "Power greater than ourselves" and "God *as we understood Him.*" In Step Seven Bill deleted the words "on our knees," and he altered his introductory statement. Concerning the approach he employed, Bill later commented:

> Who first suggested the actual compromise words
> I do not know, but they are words well known

throughout the length and breadth of A.A. today: In Step Two we decided to describe God as a "Power greater than ourselves." In Steps Three and Eleven we inserted the words "God *as we understood Him.*" From Step Seven we deleted the expression "on our knees." And, as a lead-in sentence to all the steps we wrote these words: "Here are the steps we took which are suggested as a Program of Recovery." A.A.'s Twelve Steps were to be *suggestions* only.

Such were the final concessions to those of little or no faith; this was the great contribution of our atheists and agnostics. They had widened our gateway so that all who suffer might pass through, regardless of their belief or *lack of belief.*

God was certainly there in our steps, but He was now expressed in terms that anybody—*anybody at all*—could accept and try. Countless A.A.'s have since testified that without this great evidence of liberality they never could have set foot on any path of spiritual progress or even approached us in the first place. It was another one of those providential ten-strikes.[4]

After Wilson completed his book, he and his colleagues directed that 400 copies be printed and sent to everyone who might be concerned with the problem of alcoholism. Hoping for approval from the religious community, Bill sent copies to Dr. Harry Emerson Fosdick, a powerful leader of Protestantism, and to the Catholic Committee on Publications in the New York Roman Catholic Archdiocese. Dr. Fosdick expressed deep appreciation for the volume. The Catholic Committee made some suggestions for improvement and one for change. They requested the author to change "Heaven" to "Utopia" in the first chapter's sentence, "We have found Heaven right here on this good old earth." Bill made the suggested change.

Given the title *Alcoholics Anonymous,* the corrected manuscript went to the printers. Five thousand copies were published in April of 1939. It got the name "Big Book" because of the original volume's bulky size.

Bill Wilson himself suggested compelling reasons for characterizing his program as the Twelve Step Spiritual Program of Recovery. In an address to the St. Louis A.A. convention he referred to the steps as "Twelve Steps of recovery" and as spiritual principles:

> Unless each A.A. member follows to the best of his ability our suggested Twelve Steps of recovery, he almost certainly signs his own death warrant. Drunkenness and disintegration are not penalties inflicted by people in authority; they are results of personal disobedience to spiritual principles. We *must* obey certain principles, or we die.[5]

Bill Wilson's final wording of his Twelve Step Program, initially published in the first edition of *Alcoholics Anonymous*, is the formulation quoted in the introduction of this book.

1. *'Pass It On': The Story of Bill Wilson and How the A.A. Message Reached the World* (New York: Alcoholics Anonymous World Services, Inc., 1984), 198–99.
2. Ernest Kurtz, *Not-God: A History of Alcoholics Anonymous* (Center City, MN: Hazelden, 1979), 70.
3. [William G. Wilson], *Alcoholics Anonymous Comes of Age* (New York: Alcoholics Anonymous Publishing, Inc., 1957), 163.
4. Ibid., 167.
5. Ibid., 119.

Chapter 3

Influences of the Oxford Group on the Twelve Steps

Oxford Group Leaders

Bill W.'s design of the Twelve Steps grew out of his relationship with the Oxford Group Movement and especially with the Reverend Samuel Moor Shoemaker (1893–1963), rector of Calvary Episcopal Church in New York City and, until 1941, the American leader of the Oxford Groups. By his association with Oxford Groupers and Sam Shoemaker personally and by practicing Oxford Group principles, Bill began his recovery from alcoholism and never again drank alcoholic beverages.

The Reverend Frank Buchman (1887–1961), a Lutheran pastor, founded the Oxford Group Movement in America early in the 20th century. Initially called The First Century Christian Fellowship, in the late 1930s it also came to be known as Moral Re-Armament. To understand the thought and practice of the Oxford Groups is to understand the principles that Bill W. incorporated into the Twelve Steps.

Oxford Group's Distinctive Beliefs and Practices

The Oxford Group aimed to be an interdenominational movement dedicated to radically changing people's lives. Oxford Groupers emphasized that change came by following definite principles. Individuals could have a life-altering conversion experience by surrendering themselves to God for forgiveness and guidance, by confessing their sins to God and others, by making restitution for wrongs done, and by providing personal witness of their changed lives for the purpose of changing others.

To assist in this conversion experience, a person called a life-changer or a "soul surgeon," introduced seekers to the "Five C's" of Confidence, Confession, Conviction, Conversion, and Continuance. First, the life-changer won the *confidence* of the prospective convert, usually by showing friendliness and concern. Next, he called upon the person to acknowledge his sin and to *confess* his sins very specifically. The life-changer accomplished step two by sharing something of his own sin and success in achieving change in his life. In turn, the life-changer urged the prospective convert to make a public confession to help others and to reinforce his own place on the road to conversion. *Conviction* followed confession. Groupers described it as the inward certainty of the seriousness of sin and the desire to be free from its power.

Called the "miracle of God's spirit," *conversion* came after conviction. It involved the surrender of the person's will to God and the commitment to hear and obey guidance received from God. In turn, conversion generated restitution. Participants were expected to exert some effort to make up for the wrongs they had done. Finally, in the interest of *continuance* changed persons took part in the fellowship of the group and worked to change others as they had been changed.

An equally distinctive component of the Oxford Group Movement was the "house party" concept. Small and large groups of people gathered together at a home or a hotel for a weekend or a week. In this retreatlike setting group sessions took place, providing life-changers opportunity to relate to the guests on a one-on-one basis, in order to change their lives in Oxford Group style.

Ambivalent Relationship to Christianity

Oxford Groupers sometimes spoke of the cross and the power of the cross. For example, Frank Buchman would quote 1 John 1:7(KJV), "The blood of Jesus Christ His Son cleanseth us from all sin," but he seemed to speak of the cross of Christ as a power that saves the world without saying explicitly what the Gospel is and how it works. One of Buchman's speeches highlights his Christ-centered viewpoint:

> We are in a global effort to win the world to our Lord and Savior, Jesus Christ. Then the great truths of the Gospel will once more become great and Jesus Christ will be King. There is your ideology. It is the whole message of our Lord and Saviour Jesus Christ. The message in its entirety is the only last hope that will save the world. The only hope. Our only answer. Go forth with that message united and you will save the world.[1]

On another occasion, however, Buchman spoke in anything but Christian terms about life-changing power. Characterizing the nature of the Oxford Group Movement, Buchman said:

> You may say spiritual revolution if you want to, or you may say Christian revolution, or you can put it in any qualification or terms you like. Our aim is the remaking of the world. We remake people; nations are remade.[2]

Willard Hunter, an associate of Frank Buchman, has offered an explanation for Buchman's dissimilar positions. Hunter insists that Buchman personally was fully devoted to Christianity, but, at the same time, he was dedicated to remaking the world by whatever power it could be done:

> He was totally committed to the religion of his own heritage. His announced aim was to usher in "the greatest revolution of all time whereby the Cross of Christ will transform the world." But if his Confucian friends or communist friends did not see it this way right off, he was resolved that theoretical differences would not separate him from those who could help remake the globe.
>
> In the back of his mind there was another thought: Since Christ was God's true manifestation on earth, the Buddhists and the others would find out about that in

due course, by revelation, as they listened to God and faithfully carried out His commands. Buchman did not feel called on to superimpose his religious views. God Himself would take care of all that sort of business in His own way and in His own time.[3]

Shoemaker's Influence on the Steps

Sam Shoemaker followed in the footsteps of Frank Buchman. His ministry, too, expressed the ambiguity of the Oxford Group message. He preached Christ-centered sermons at Calvary Church, proclaiming salvation through the atoning work of Jesus Christ. In one sermon Shoemaker became quite specific:

> Jesus Christ went up on the cross for you and for me. He would have done it if there had been no other sinner in the universe but you or me. "He died that we might be forgiven." The Cross cleared the way back to God. His death atoned for human sin. The apparatus of forgiveness is there.[4]

Although Shoemaker preached the Christian Gospel at worship services on Sunday morning, he spoke differently at Oxford Group meetings. At these meetings, in keeping with Oxford Group practice, Shoemaker encouraged people to surrender as much of themselves as they could to as much of God as they understood. In his treatise *How to Find God* Shoemaker gave an example of his Oxford Group approach:

> Come to the ultimate [sic] Sum of things with an honest appraisal of yourself. Throw yourself upon that Ultimate Sum of things with an honest search, with honest desire to be different, with wide-open readiness to receive any message that comes to you. Give as much of yourself as you can to as much of God as you understand . . . God will come through to you and make Himself known."[5]

Shoemaker readily gave generic religious advice because he believed, like Buchman, that whoever approached God according to his knowledge and ability would ultimately be led by God to find "the God and Father of our Lord Jesus Christ." His sermon, "The Christian's Victory," illustrates this confidence:

> Come to whatever God there is, whether you know Him yet or not, and surrender your sin and yourself to the Ultimate Truth about this universe. As you do this, and as your attempt to come to God will be met far more than halfway by God coming out toward you, you will realize that the "God and Father of our Lord Jesus Christ" is precisely what you are talking about when you say words like "the Ultimate Truth about this universe" so that when you surrender yourself to God, you find yourself back in the old familiar outlook of the Christian religion.[6]

Consistent with Oxford Group teaching, Shoemaker believed that each person has the inborn ability to surrender one's self and one's sin to God in order to receive God's forgiveness and life-transforming power. He taught that when a person surrenders self to God, God does what only God can do. He works conversion with all its blessings. Shoemaker stated this position clearly in his book, *With the Holy Spirit and with Fire:*

> We do not convert ourselves: the Grace of God is the primary factor. But we can hold out on the Grace of God, or we can welcome Him in. Our willingness to surrender as much of ourselves as we can to as much of Christ as we understand may be our first step in the experiment of faith. This beginning of self-surrender is our part in our own conversion, and helps to bring us into the stream.[7]

A comparison of Oxford Group teachings with the Twelve Steps readily demonstrates that Bill W. and other recovering alcoholics learned the principles incorporated into the Twelve Steps from Oxford Group leader Sam Shoemaker. In the early days of their sobriety, they drafted six statements, on which Bill W. would later base Twelve Steps. These six statements

contain the principles they had employed in achieving and
maintaining sobriety:

1. We admitted that we were licked, that we were
   powerless over alcohol.
2. We made an inventory of our defects or sins.
3. We confessed or shared our shortcomings with
   another person in confidence.
4. We made restitution to all those we had harmed by
   our drinking.
5. We tried to help other alcoholics, with no thought
   of reward in money or prestige.
6. We prayed to whatever God we thought there was
   for power to practice these precepts.[8]

At the 20th anniversary A.A. convention in St. Louis, Wilson noted several key concepts A.A. had learned from Shoemaker:

> The early A.A. got its ideas of self-examination,
> acknowledgment of character defects, restitution for
> harm done, and working with others straight from the
> Oxford Groups and directly from Sam Shoemaker,
> their former leader in America and from nowhere
> else.[9]

Additional Oxford Group teachings Wilson learned from
Shoemaker are found in Bill's conversations with Ebby
Thatcher, who, earlier than Bill, benefited from the tutelage
of Sam Shoemaker. We recall, for example, that Ebby told Bill
the Oxford Group taught him he should try to pray to whatever God he thought there was to help him carry out the
group precepts, and if he did not believe in a God, to experi-
ment with praying to whatever God he thought there might
possibly be. In his talks with Bill, Ebby spoke of God as
"another power" and as "a higher power."

Shoemaker: A.A. Cofounder

So influential was Dr. Sam Shoemaker on the founding of
Alcoholics Anonymous that Bill W. was not at all reluctant to

speak of him as an A.A. cofounder. In a letter to Shoemaker in 1963, just six months before Shoemaker died, Bill wrote:

> Certainly there were other indispensable contributions without which we should have probably got noplace [sic]. But none of these were so large or so critical as your own. Though I wish the "co-founder" tag had never been hitched to any of us, I have no hesitancy in adding your name to the list![10]

Bill Wilson's testimony is clear. He believed Oxford Grouper Sam Shoemaker contributed more than anyone else to the spiritual principles of Alcoholics Anonymous, to the formulation of the Twelve Steps, and to Wilson's interpretation of the Steps in *Alcoholics Anonymous*.

---

1. Frank N. D. Buchman, *Remaking the World* (London: Blandford Press, 1961), 148.
2. Tom Driberg, *The Mystery of Moral Re-Armament* (New York: Alfred A. Knopf, 1965), 57.
3. T. Willard Hunter, "World-Changing Through Life-Changing" (S.T.M. thesis, Andover-Newton Theological School, 1977), 115.
4. Samuel M. Shoemaker, *How to Become a Christian* (New York: Harper & Bros., Publishers, 1953), 59.
5. Samuel M. Shoemaker, *How to Find God* (c. 1958), 5–6, Shoemaker Papers, Record Group 101-43-3, Episcopal Church Archives, Austin, Texas.
6. Samuel M. Shoemaker, *Christ and This Crisis* (New York: Fleming H. Revell Co., 1943), 87–88.
7. Samuel M. Shoemaker, *With the Holy Spirit and with Fire* (New York: Harper & Row Publishers, 1960), 40.
8. [William G. Wilson], *Alcoholics Anonymous Comes of Age* (New York: Alcoholics Anonymous Publishing, Inc., 1957), 160.
9. [Wilson], *A.A. Comes of Age*, 39.
10. William G. Wilson to Samuel M. Shoemaker, 23 April 1963, Shoemaker Papers, Record Group 101-39-5, Episcopal Church Archives, Austin, Texas.

Chapter 4

Bill W.'s Explanation of Each Step

Bill Wilson not only published the Twelve Steps, but he also wrote two interpretations of the steps. The first is found in the 1939 edition of *Alcoholics Anonymous* and in successive editions. The second interpretation appeared 14 years later, in 1953, in Wilson's second book, *Twelve Steps and Twelve Traditions*.

In this chapter we shall focus on Wilson's first interpretation because the book, *Alcoholics Anonymous*, is generally regarded as A.A.'s official handbook.

Step One: *We admitted that we were powerless over alcohol that our lives had become unmanageable.*

Step Two: *Came to believe that a Power greater than ourselves could restore us to sanity.*

In *Alcoholics Anonymous* Wilson devotes less than half a page to his discussion of Steps One and Two, referring the reader back to previous chapters in the book for a fuller interpretation:

> Our description of the alcoholic, the chapter on the agnostic, and our personal adventures before and after make clear three pertinent ideas:
> (a) That we were alcoholic and could not manage our own lives.
> (b) That probably no human power could have relieved our alcoholism.
> (c) That God could and would if He were sought.[1]

Wilson discusses the alcoholic in two chapters, "There Is a Solution" and "More About Alcoholism." In "There Is a Solution" he shows that it is necessary to include religion in any discussion of a solution to alcoholism. The application of "spiritual tools" is necessary for recovery[2] because a spiritual experience is essential and God Himself must work in the heart to accomplish those things a person cannot do by his own willpower. While most A.A.s favor church membership, not all join such bodies, and it is not the concern of A.A. which religious bodies people join. All people, Wilson says, have their own way of establishing a relationship with God. Even agnosticism poses no great obstacle to a spiritual experience.

In "More About Alcoholism" Bill Wilson refers to the purpose of the First Step. It calls alcoholics to concede fully to their innermost selves that they have lost the ability to control their drinking. Alcoholism, Bill observes, is a progressive illness. The person who has it can never recover control of his drinking. Except in a few rare cases, the only defense against drinking must come from a Higher Power.

Wilson highlights the issue of agnosticism in the chapter "We Agnostics." He observes that about half of the original fellowship was atheist or agnostic, but because a spiritual basis of life is essential for recovery, they had to find a greater power than self by which to live. He writes:

> Well, that's exactly what this book is about. Its main object is to enable you to find a Power greater than yourself which will solve your problem. That means we have written a book which we believe to be spiritual as well as moral. And it means, of course, that we are going to talk about God.[3]

Wilson spells out his approach to agnosticism by reflecting on his own experience and that of his early associates. They had viewed theological systems with deep skepticism and yet, at the same time, wondered how the wonderful world came into being. He asserts that simply a willingness to believe in a greater Power brought results, even though recovering persons were not able fully to define or comprehend that Power Wilson calls God. Indeed, writes Wilson, each person may have his own concept of God, but he will discover that, whatever his concept, help is available:

Much to our relief, we discovered we did not need to consider another's conception of God. Our own conception, however inadequate, was sufficient to make the approach and to effect a contact with Him. As soon as we admitted the possible existence of a Creative Intelligence, a Spirit of the Universe underlying the totality of things, we began to be possessed of a new sense of power and direction, provided we took other simple steps. We found that God does not make too hard terms with those who seek Him. To us, the Realm of the Spirit is broad, roomy, all inclusive; never exclusive or forbidding to those who earnestly seek. It is open, we believe, to all men . . .

As soon as a man can say that he does believe, or is willing to believe, we emphatically assure him that he is on his way.[4]

In the second part of the chapter "We Agnostics" Wilson takes up the question of why a person should believe in a Power greater than one's self. He argues that while people believe in many assumptions for which there is no visual proof, it is not unusual for them to try to explain away the fact that underneath the material world and life there is an "All Powerful, Guiding Creative Intelligence."[5] Atheists and agnostics usually choose to believe that human intelligence is the last word. However, Wilson asserts, the created order demonstrates the existence of a greater Power.

Wilson appeals to atheists and agnostics to lay aside prejudice, even against organized religion, calling for tolerance. Then he applies his most persuasive argument: persons who have reached out to a greater Power of their own conception have experienced a revolutionary change in their lives. Reason is not everything. In fact, we all have a fundamental idea of God. Faith is essential; it is part of our make-up to have faith in some kind of God. "When many hundreds of people," Bill writes, "are able to say that the consciousness of the Presence of God is today the most important fact of their lives, they present a powerful reason why one should have faith."[6]

Step Three: *Made a decision to turn our will and our lives over to the care of God as we understood Him.*

Referring to Steps One and Two, Wilson writes, "Being convinced [of them], *we were at step three*, which is that we decided to turn our will and our life over to God *AS WE UNDERSTOOD HIM.*"[7] To accomplish this, he says, an alcoholic must be convinced that a life run on self-will cannot succeed. Only God can help. Thus, the alcoholic must stop playing God and name God as the director of the drama of life and as His Father. "This concept was the keystone of the new and triumphant arch through which we passed to freedom."[8]

According to Wilson the alcoholic's new position toward God produces remarkable things. The alcoholic experiences a new Employer, an interest in contributing to life, a new peace of mind, a successful stance toward life, a consciousness of God's presence, and a lack of fear of the present and future. Not surprisingly, Wilson describes this experience as a rebirth.[9]

For the implementation of Step Three Wilson proposes this prayer:

> "God, I offer myself to Thee—to build with me and to do with me as Thou wilt. Relieve me of the bondage of self, that I may better do Thy will. Take away my difficulties, that victory over them may bear witness to those I would help of Thy Power, Thy Love, and Thy Way of life. May I do Thy will always!"[10]

He advises taking the Third Step with an understanding person, perhaps a spouse, friend, or spiritual advisor.

Step Four: *Made a searching and fearless moral inventory of ourselves.*

Bill Wilson presents Step Four as launching a course of vigorous action to perpetuate and reinforce sobriety and to produce a quality life of sobriety. Dubbing it a step of personal housekeeping or honest taking of stock, he says its intent is to search out the flaws that have caused personal failure.

Resentment, he emphasizes, is the "number one" offender that destroys more alcoholics than anything else. From it stem all kinds of spiritual disease that must be overcome in the interest of mental and physical health.

He suggests setting resentments down on paper, listing the people, institutions, or principles that are the object of anger. Speaking about himself, he observes that "in most cases it was found that our self-esteem, our pocketbooks, our ambitions, our personal relationships (including sex) were hurt or threatened."[11] He urges thoroughness and honesty because resentment threatens "the maintenance and growth of a spiritual experience."[12] Such feelings shut people off from the sunlight of the Spirit.

Wilson describes a way to deal with injurious people: Treat them like sick persons, avoid retaliation or argument, and be kindly and tolerant. Recovering alcoholics must recognize their own mistakes—their dishonesty, selfishness, self-seeking, and fearfulness. The value of listing faults honestly and being willing to set matters straight with the help of God cannot be overemphasized. In conclusion, Wilson urges his readers to examine their sexual wrongs and to include them in the inventory for confession and amendment.

Step Five: *Admitted to God, to ourselves, and to another human being, the exact nature of our wrongs.*

For his discussion of Steps Five through Eleven, Wilson begins a new chapter, "Into Action." At the outset he acknowledges that he has been discussing what is involved in getting a new relationship with God and in discovering obstacles in the path. Step Four, taking a personal inventory, helps to identify those obstacles. Step Five uses the inventory to admit "to God, to ourselves, and to another human being, the exact nature of our defects."[13] The omission of this step, Wilson believes, might prevent the conquest of drinking.

Taking the Fifth Step, recounting one's life story, produces humility, fearlessness, and honesty. It is important, however, to find the right listener, possibly an ordained minister, an understanding friend, a doctor, a psychologist, or a family member.

For Wilson taking Step Five marks the beginning of a spiritual experience. He writes:

We may have had certain spiritual beliefs, but now we begin to have a spiritual experience. The feelings that the drink problem has disappeared will often come strongly. We feel we are on the Broad Highway, walking hand in hand with the Spirit of the Universe.[14]

Step Six: *Were entirely ready to have God remove all these defects of character.*

Step Seven: *Humbly asked Him to remove our shortcomings.*

In the "Big Book" Bill Wilson devotes only two paragraphs to Steps Six and Seven. He focuses on "willingness" as the key to understanding Step Six, because willingness is indispensable to approaching God for the removal of defects. He advises his readers to ask God for willingness that might be lacking and proposes this prayer for humbly asking God to remove personal shortcomings:

My Creator, I am now willing that you should have all of me, good and bad. I pray that you now remove from me every single defect of character which stands in the way of my usefulness to you and my fellows. Grant me strength, as I go out from here, to do your bidding. Amen.[15]

Step Eight: *Made a list of all persons we had harmed, and became willing to make amends to them all.*

Step Nine: *Made direct amends to such people whenever possible, except when to do so would injure them or others.*

In his first commentary Bill Wilson treats Steps Eight and Nine together. Step Eight stresses the importance of making a list of all persons the recovering alcoholic has harmed and of becoming willing to make amends to all of them. Step Nine naturally follows, the actual making of amends when it is appropriate to do so. Actually, the moral inventory of Step Four, includes composing an amends list, which becomes the basis for making amends for harm done to others. Wilson considers this step as essential to sobriety:

Now we go out to our fellows and repair the damage done in the past . . . If we haven't the will to do this, we ask until it comes. Remember it was agreed at the beginning *we would go to any lengths for victory over alcohol.*[16]

Wilson emphasizes the purpose for taking these steps: "To fit ourselves to be of maximum service to God and the people about us."[17] He recognizes that in some cases it might be wise not to announce the spiritual or religious motivation for personal amendment, but simply to demonstrate "a sincere desire to set right the wrong."[18] This would be true especially if an individual "still smarts from injustice to him."[19] Wilson never encourages, however, shying away from the subject of God. Rather, when it will serve any good purpose, "we are willing to announce our convictions with tact and common sense."[20]

Wilson advises how to approach an enemy in making amendment, admitting that such a task is difficult but nonetheless beneficial. "We go to him in a helpful and forgiving spirit, confessing our former ill feeling and expressing our regret."[21] "Simply tell him," Wilson adds, "we will never get over our drinking until we have done our utmost to straighten out our past."[22] And he observes that in 9 cases out of 10 the unexpected happens: the enemy admits his own fault and reconciliation follows. Even when it does not, the alcoholic has done his part. Above all, the alcoholic is to pray for strength and direction to do the right thing no matter what the personal consequences may be. Bill goes so far as to say, "We may lose our position or reputation or face jail, but we are willing. We have to be. We must not shrink at anything."[23]

Wilson expresses concern that other people should be considered in the practice of Step Eight. He urges the alcoholic "not to be the hasty and foolish martyr who would needlessly sacrifice others to save himself from the alcoholic pit."[24] He advises against taking drastic action that might implicate others without securing their consent. In the matter of sexual unfaithfulness Wilson advocates caution in telling a spouse what was unknown to him or her. Though there may be exceptions, it is probably better not to identify a sexual partner in making amendment. "We are sorry for what we have done," he writes," and, God willing, it shall not be repeated. More than that we cannot do; we have no right to go further."[25] He emphatically states that the family is to be a primary concern for the alcoholic who is making amends. "The spiritual life is not a theory. *We have to live it*,"[26] he notes, while also cautioning that the alcoholic not urge the spiritual principles of life upon his family until they express a desire to live according to them. In conclusion Wilson notes that some people have to be dealt with by letter and that some wrongs can perhaps never be righted. Nevertheless, practicing Steps Eight and Nine will result in freedom, security, happiness, and a realization of God's enabling power in life.

Step Ten: *Continued to take personal inventory and when we were wrong promptly admitted it.*

Wilson considers Step Ten as the world of the Spirit where the practitioner will grow in understanding and effectiveness over an entire lifetime. He urges his readers "to continue to take personal inventory and continue to set right any new mistakes as we go along."[27] Recovering alcoholics must watch for selfishness, dishonesty, resentment, and fear; they must ask God to remove these as soon as discovered; they must discuss them with someone; they must make amends quickly if someone has been harmed and reach out to help someone else. Love and tolerance toward others are especially important.

In his explanation of Step Ten Wilson addresses the recovering person's new attitude toward liquor. For the alcoholic the time of sanity has returned, bringing a new freedom from liquor that he views as his own without personal thought or effort. Since there is no cure for alcoholism, such a new posture will continue as long as a fit spiritual condition is maintained. Thus it is important daily to seek and do God's will and to exercise the fullest measure of willpower in the fulfillment of this goal. Wilson becomes almost mystical. "We have begun to sense the flow of His Spirit into us. To some extent we have become God-conscious. We have begun to develop this vital sixth sense."[28]

Step Eleven: *Sought through prayer and meditation to improve our conscious contact with God AS WE UNDERSTOOD HIM, praying only for knowledge of His will for us and the power to carry that out.*

Bill Wilson begins his comments on Step Eleven with a discussion of prayer and meditation. Prayer works if the one who prays has the proper attitude and works at prayer. He advocates both evening and morning prayer. In the evening, review the day, ask God's forgiveness, and inquire of Him what corrective measures need to be taken. In the morning, ask God to direct one's thinking toward the 24 hours ahead. Wilson advises that, if decisions need to be made, ask God for inspiration, an intuitive thought, or a decision. Conclude the period of meditation with the prayer that God will guide each step through the day and give freedom from self-will and selfishness.

According to Wilson one need not meditate alone and without resources. He recommends the companionship of spouses or friends and the use of one's religious denominational materials or other selected prayers. He recommends priests, ministers, and rabbis as available resources.

Wilson encourages prayer throughout the day. Praying to know God's will and to obey it repels harmful excitement, fear, anger, worry, self-pity, or foolish decisions. It makes for more efficient living.

Step Twelve: *Having had a spiritual awakening as the result of these steps, we tried to carry this message to alcoholics, and to practice these principles in all our affairs.*

Bill W. devotes an entire chapter to Step Twelve. Entitling the chapter, "Working With Others," he begins with his major premise: "Practical experience shows that nothing will so much insure immunity from drinking as intensive work with other alcoholics. It works when other activities fail."[29] Alcoholics who carry the message to other alcoholics help themselves and also give help to others that no one else can. He sees contacts with newcomers and other A.A. members as some of life's "bright spots."

Referrals from doctors, ministers, priests, or hospitals give A.A. members opportunity to work with alcoholics. While A.A. members may learn much from ministers and doctors, they are not to be evangelists or reformers. Rather, they are to cooperate with ministers and doctors as having something special to offer from their own drinking experience.

Wilson offers additional advice. Become acquainted with possible prospects for Alcoholics Anonymous. Recognize the alcoholic as a sick person. If he does not want to stop drinking, do not waste time trying to persuade him, lest you spoil a later opportunity. If, on the other hand, he does want to stop drinking, talk with the person most interested in him, usually the spouse. Get to know as much about the alcoholic as possible. Do not talk with him when he is intoxicated, but wait for the end of a drinking spree or for a lucid moment. When the alcoholic indicates willingness to receive help, then share your own recovery experience with that person. Give him a copy of the book *Alcoholics Anonymous*. If he is hospitalized, visit him. Whenever and wherever you visit, visit him by yourself. Tell him about your own experience of drinking and recovery and encourage him to talk. If he is alcoholic, he will understand as you talk with him about alcoholism as an illness and the hope of a solution. Tell him about the inadequacy of willpower for recovery. Stress the spiritual feature, that he must "*be willing to believe in a Power greater than himself and that he live by spiritual principles*,"[30] that is, put into action religious beliefs he may have or those general principles espoused by A.A. and common to most denominations. Be sure the alcoholic knows he is under no obligation to you but obligated only to help other alcoholics when he escapes his own difficulties. Finally, he advises, "Never talk down to an alcoholic from any moral or spiritual hilltop; simply lay out the kit of spiritual tools for his inspection. Show him how they worked for you."[31]

Wilson emphasizes that the A.A. member should not push or prod the alcoholic or be discouraged if the prospect does not immediately respond. Rather, he should begin work on others and give the initial prospect time to make a better decision about his drinking. However, when visiting on a prospect a second time, the A.A. member should offer to help him work through the Twelve Steps and to provide help for his family also.

1 [William G. Wilson et al], *Alcoholics Anonymous*, rev. 2d ed. (New York: Alcoholics Anonymous Publishing, Inc., 1955), 60.

2. Ibid, 25.

3. Ibid, 45.

4. Ibid, 46-47.

5. Ibid, 49.

6. Ibid, 51.

7. Ibid, 60.

8. Ibid, 62.

9. Ibid, 63.

10. Ibid.

11. Ibid, 64–65.

12. Ibid, 66.

13. Ibid, 72.

14. Ibid, 75.

15. Ibid, 76.

16. Ibid.

17. Ibid, 77.

18. Ibid.

19. Ibid.

20. Ibid.

21. Ibid.

22. Ibid.

23. Ibid, 79.

24. Ibid.

25. Ibid, 81.

26. Ibid, 83.

27. Ibid, 84.

28. Ibid, 85.

29. Ibid, 89.

30. Ibid, 93.

31. Ibid, 95.

Part 2

*The Twelve Steps—
Challenge for the Church*

Chapter 5

The Challenge for a
Biblical Response

Disregard of Christianity's Central Teaching

An examination of the origins of the Twelve Steps readily reveals the principal source of Bill Wilson's recovery principles. He derived his Twelve Step Spiritual Program of Recovery chiefly from the teachings and practices of the Oxford Group Movement. These teachings and practices, in turn, were rooted in the Christian tradition. Both Oxford Group teachings and Twelve Step principles express a variety of Biblical ideas, yet both seriously disregard the central teaching of Christianity. What is Christianity's primary teaching? That God forgives people's sins and declares them right with Him solely by His grace through faith in Jesus Christ as Savior. God does this because Jesus, His Son, has made good for our sins by His sinless life and His innocent death on the cross.

St. Paul speaks extensively of this central teaching of the Christian faith in his New Testament letters. Writing to the Romans, Paul says that God declares people righteous through faith in Jesus Christ, that is, He justifies us:

> No one will be declared righteous in [God's] sight by observing the law; rather, through the law we become conscious of sin. But now a righteousness from God, apart from the law, has been made known, to which the Law and the Prophets testify. This righteousness from God comes through faith in Jesus Christ to all who believe. There is no difference, for all have sinned and fall short of the glory of God, and are justified freely by his grace through the redemption that came by Christ Jesus. God presented him as a sacri-

fice of atonement, through faith in his blood (Rom. 3:20–25).

In a similar way in his letter to the Galatians, Paul emphasizes that no one can be justified before God by relying on obedience to God's Law. No one can possibly live up to God's requirements.

> All who rely on observing the law are under a curse, for it is written: "Cursed is everyone who does not continue to do everything written in the Book of Law." Clearly no one is justified before God by the law, because, "The righteous will live by faith." The law is not based on faith; on the contrary, "The man who does these things will live by them." Christ redeemed us from the curse of the law by becoming a curse for us, for it is written: "Cursed is everyone who is hung on a tree." He redeemed us in order that the blessing given to Abraham might come to the Gentiles through Christ Jesus, so that by faith we might receive the promise of the Spirit (Gal. 3:10–14).

When the central teaching of Scripture is set aside, there is no Christianity. Then no other Bible teaching can be correctly understood or applied.

The disregard of the Steps for the Bible's chief teaching of God's forgiving grace in Jesus Christ gives critics reason to condemn the Twelve Steps as *entirely* unacceptable and spiritually destructive to all persons practicing them. These critics remind us that the steps speak of God as "Higher Power" and refer to Him as God *as we understood Him.* In addition, the steps imply that all is well between a person and God when the individual begins to turn his will and life over to the care of whatever God he understands there to be.

Total Rejection Not the Answer

As we have already noted, Martin and Deidre Bobgan exemplify the approach that totally rejects the steps in their book *12 Steps to Destruction.* The following excerpt illustrates their viewpoint: "Most systems of codependency and addiction recovery are based upon various psychological counseling theories and therapies and upon the religious and philosophical teachings of Alcoholics Anonymous (AA). In short, such programs are based upon the wisdom of man and the worship of false gods."[1]

In another place in the same book the Bobgans have written, "If Jesus is truly the answer to life's problems and indeed the very source of life, why are both non-Christians and Christians looking for answers elsewhere?"[2]

The Bobgans express truth. They fail to understand, however, that all people are spiritually incapable of restoring themselves to God by reaching out to Jesus. We cannot expect people, using their own reason or strength, to look to Jesus for answers to the problems in their lives. Therefore, we cannot reject the steps simply by saying that Jesus is the answer to life's problems and everyone should turn to Him. Nor can we dismiss the steps as having no value because they are based on the wisdom of man and wrong understandings of God. Rather, we need to see if the steps can be useful in preparing people for the Christian message and if the steps can give earthly blessings to those who use them.

Noncritical Approach Not the Answer

While some evaluators see no value at all in the steps, other Christian writers encourage the use of the steps and identify in them Christian good that is not there. They offer Christian interpretations and applications of the steps, but tend to do so without seriously dealing with shortcomings and dangers of the steps and without advocating a realistic and forthright biblical appraisal.

Illustrative of the noncritical approach are books by Dennis Morreim, Michele S. Matto, and J. Keith Miller. First, in *The Road to Recovery* Dennis Morreim emphasizes that A.A. and the church travel on parallel roads and share common ground.

> AA and the church are parallel roads, traveling the same direction, covering similar terrain, yet consistently maintaining their distance . . .

Though there are differences in these parallel roads, there are places along the way where both AA and the Christian church have some common ground. This is so evident that no one has to search for hidden themes upon which both may converse. The common ground is in the words *grace, message, power, and change* (transformation).

Both AA and the church proclaim the grace of God.[3]

Second, Michele S. Matto, in *The 12 Steps in the Bible*, says the steps express the church's traditional beliefs.

We who are in Twelve Step programs are a group of people who have already been brought to our knees by life's circumstances, and who are truly motivated to begin the deepening life of prayer. The Twelve Steps are nothing more and nothing less than what the church has been about all these centuries.[4]

Finally, in *A Hunger for Healing* J. Keith Miller says that by working the steps people find a loving and redeeming God, the same God Christians confess.

In the Twelve Steps one finds out what God is like by entering a community of people who have made a radical commitment of their lives to God. As newcomers see God working in the lives of people in that community, they learn about his nature and how he operates. As they work the Steps and put their own lives in the hands of God (whatever they call God at first) they discover firsthand the loving, redeeming, supporting, moral and confronting nature of God. Later many of them see that this is in fact the same God that Christians believe in, and numbers of them join the Church.[5]

Our Goal: Biblical Assessment

Even though some see value in the Twelve Steps, the steps continue to challenge the church to provide a sound biblical response to their principles. To assess the steps, using the

Bible, first we must search for and identify biblical teachings suitable for crafting a response, and, second, we must try to apply these scriptural resources fairly, neither rejecting the steps unnecessarily nor accepting them noncritically. In doing so, we will be able to see how God uses the Twelve Steps in His care of persons.

---

1. Martin and Deidre Bobgan, *12 Steps to Destruction* (Santa Barbara, CA: EastGate Publishers, 1991), 5.

2. Ibid., 7.

3. Dennis C. Morreim, *The Road to Recovery: Bridges Between the Bible and the Twelve Steps* (Minneapolis: Augsburg, 1990), 133.

4. Michele S. Matto, *The Twelve Steps in the Bible* (New York: Paulist Press, 1991), 9.

5. J. Keith Miller, *A Hunger for Healing: The Twelve Steps as a Classic Model for Christian Spiritual Growth* (San Francisco: Harper, 1991), xiii.

Chapter 6

A Biblical Evaluation of the Twelve Steps

Three Teachings

The Bible provides ample resources for meeting the challenge set before us: to evaluate the steps, using biblical teachings. We shall explore three resources, one by one, to discover how they relate to one another to shape our response. The first scriptural teaching we shall examine is the doctrine of the natural knowledge of God, that is, what people can know about God by their own abilities, apart from His revelation in Scripture.

Natural Knowledge of God

There is good reason to begin with this doctrine. The Twelve Step principles are far enough removed from the heart and center of the Christian faith that the steps appear to stem from the natural knowledge of God rather than from the teachings of the Oxford Group, a movement with Christian origins. As we shall discover, what the steps prescribe could readily derive from what people can know about God apart from Scripture. This means a study of the natural knowledge of God is essential in assessing the steps from the Bible's point of view.

The Bible clearly teaches that people can know something about God, apart from God's special revelation in Scripture. In his letter to the Romans St. Paul has much to say about the natural knowledge of God, that is, the inborn knowledge we have as human beings. At the outset he talks about how this knowledge comes to human beings. First, we can know about God from *His creative work.* In Rom. 1:20 Paul writes, "Since the creation of the world God's invisible qualities—his eternal power and divine nature—have been clearly seen, being understood from what has been made, so that men are without excuse."

In the second chapter of Romans, the apostle adds that *God's Law written in human hearts*, known as natural law, also contributes to our natural knowledge of God. That law causes people's consciences to accuse them or affirm them for what they do. In verses 14 and 15 he observes that "when Gentiles, who do not have the law, do by nature things required by the law, they are a law for themselves, even though they do not have the law, since they show that the requirements of the law are written on their hearts, their consciences also bearing witness, and their thoughts now accusing, now even defending them."

Finally, Paul recognizes that people can know about God, apart from revelation, by *God's continuous working in the realms of nature and human history*. On the occasion of a visit to Lystra, St. Paul stated that "He [God] has not left himself without testimony: He has shown kindness by giving you rain from heaven and crops in their seasons; he provides you with plenty of food and fills your hearts with joy" (Acts 14:17). In turn, while visiting Athens, Paul commented on God's activity in history: "From one man he made every nation of men, that they should inhabit the whole earth; and he determined the times set for them and the exact places where they should live. God did this so that men would seek him and perhaps reach out for him and find him though he is not far from each one of us. 'For in him we live and move and have our being'" (Acts 17:26–28).

Expressing biblical thought, two historic confessional writings of the church comment on the relationship of natural law and the natural knowledge of God. They observe that natural law, or our inborn understanding of God's will for our lives, substantially contributes to the natural knowledge of God. The one document, The Apology of the Augsburg Confession, says "human reason naturally understands the law since it has the same judgment naturally written in the mind."[1] The second document, The Formula of Concord, states much the same thing and adds that natural man also has a "dim spark of the knowledge that there is a God, as well as of the teaching of the law."[2]

A Christian teacher, Dr. Francis Pieper, summarized what people can learn about God from natural knowledge. He observed: "Man knows by nature not only that there is a personal, eternal, and almighty God, the Creator, Preserver, and Ruler of the universe, but also that this God is holy and just, who demands and rewards the good and condemns and punishes the evil."[3]

In a Christian instruction book, Edward W. A. Koehler sets forth a more extensive statement about the contents of the natural knowledge of God. His comment appears specially relevant because he uses the A.A. name for God, Higher Power. Koehler writes:

> There is no people, however rude and uncivilized, that does not believe in the existence of some Higher Power or Supreme Being. This truth is forced upon every rational being by the "creation of the world." Though God Himself is invisible to our eyes, He manifests Himself in the wonderful works of nature, for as there is no house without a builder, so there can be no created world without a Creator. It is foolish to assume that the things we see about us in nature came into existence by themselves, and that evolution and blind chance developed this well-ordered universe with its myriads of animate and inanimate beings. Thus nature proves the *existence* of God. It also proves that He is *eternal*, because He must have been before the world was made; that He is *powerful* because He made this world out of nothing; that He is a *living* God, because there could be no life in the world without Him; that He is *wise*, because each creature, from the smallest to the greatest, is so constructed as to serve its purpose effectively. Whatever we see in nature proclaims the glory of God . . .

The Gentiles, who never read the Bible, feel that there is some Higher Being that does not approve of their evil deeds, but will punish them. Thus they show that by nature they have some knowledge of the existence of God. To appease His wrath and to escape His punishment they have invented all sorts of services and sacrifices. Without this innate knowledge of God we simply could not explain why all people have some form of religion. This natural knowledge of God is true as far as it goes, but it is not perfect; it does not tell us *who* this God is, what He has done for our salvation, and how we should serve Him. The mere fact that a person believes that there is a God, does not save him.[4]

While the natural knowledge of God enables persons to know that a Higher Power exists who is powerful, wise, holy, and just, it does not reveal that God forgives sins *only* for Jesus' sake. They can deduce, however, the Higher Power is good, as St. Paul describes Him in Acts 14:17. To the people of Lystra he said of God, "He has shown kindness by giving you rain from heaven and crops in their seasons; he provides you with plenty of food and fills your hearts with joy." Furthermore, people can even come to believe, erroneously of course, that they can obtain forgiveness of sins and a right relationship with God by doing the works of the Law. In the words of Edmund Schlink, a Christian scholar, they may adhere to that belief of man's "natural religion, whose essence consists in beguiling men with an illusion of fellowship and peace with God apart from the atonement procured by Christ's blood."[5] This was certainly true of the Pharisee in Jesus' parable of the Pharisee and the tax collector. Jesus said the Pharisee exemplified people depending on their own righteousness to be acceptable to God (Luke 18:9–14). One of the traditional confessional documents of the church already quoted says it this way:

> Human reason naturally admires them [works]; because it sees only works and neither looks at nor understands faith, it dreams that the merit of these

works brings forgiveness of sins and justification. This legalistic opinion clings by nature to the minds of men, and it cannot be driven out unless we are divinely taught.[6]

Unquestionably, the natural knowledge of God provides valuable information about God and the relationship between God and people. On their part, people can interpret facets of this limited information either accurately or inaccurately. For example, persons drawing on the natural knowledge of God may accurately recognize that God is wise, powerful, and good, but as we have observed, wrongly believe they obtain God's forgiving love by obeying His laws. The various aspects of the natural knowledge of God support the proposition that the Twelve Steps *could have been derived* from the natural knowledge of God rather than from Oxford Group teachings, rooted in the Christian tradition.

Ability to Perform Outward Good Works

Now these questions present themselves: How can human beings, whose sin separates them from God and who know nothing more of God than what the natural knowledge of God supplies, possibly be able to apply that natural knowledge? In other words, can people who know no more of God than the Twelve Step Program teaches possibly practice those Twelve Steps? Again, the Bible gives us an answer. It instructs us that people separated from God can respond to their natural knowledge of God and His will and outwardly do what His Law prescribes.

These works are described as "outward good works" because they are done by those not yet spiritually alive through faith in Christ. Outward good works are not of the same value before God as works done by people forgiven and being renewed through faith in Jesus Christ. The writer to the Hebrews affirms that "without faith it is impossible to please God" (11:6). In turn, St. Paul observes that the works that truly please God are those done by people who are "God's workmanship, created in Christ Jesus to do good works," those "which God prepared in advance for us to do" (Eph. 2:10). Such works are of special worth before God because they are motivated and empowered by a faith relationship with Jesus Christ. Yet, by God's goodness, "outward good works" truly accomplish much good for people in day-to-day living on planet earth.

St. Paul recognizes people's freedom of the will to do "outward good works." In his letter to the Romans, he notes that those "who do not have the law, do by nature things required by the law, . . . they show that the requirements of the law are written on their hearts" (Rom. 2:14–15). Paul emphatically states that, apart from Christ, people are dead in sins, alienated from God, and thus have no freedom of the will in spiritual matters (Eph. 2:1; 4:18). Nevertheless, he affirms that, apart from Christ, people can indeed comply outwardly with the Law of God written in their hearts. Christian teachers have sometimes spoken of the works this compliance produces as "civilly good works."

Applying Paul's instruction, the Apology of the Augsburg Confession offers some concrete examples of how people, not yet spiritually alive to God, can use their freedom of the will outwardly to obey God's Law inscribed in their hearts:

> We are not denying freedom to the human will. The human will has freedom to choose among the works and things which reason by itself can grasp. To some extent it can achieve civil righteousness or the righteousness of works. It can talk about God and express its worship of him in outward works. It can obey rulers and parents. Externally, it can choose to keep the hands from murder, adultery, or theft. Since human nature still has reason and judgment about the things that the senses can grasp, it also retains a choice in these things, as well as the liberty and ability to achieve civil righteousness . . .
>
> Although we concede to free will the liberty and ability to do the outward works of the law, we do not ascribe to it the spiritual capacity for true fear of God,

true faith in God, true knowledge and trust that God considers, hears and forgives us.[7]

God's Left-Hand Rule

A serious question remains: Can people who live according to principles gained from the natural knowledge of God expect their obedience to result in life-enriching benefits? Specifically, can people who work the Twelve Steps expect help for overcoming addictive lifestyles? Here again we turn to the Bible for an answer. Paul's words that people use the Law written in their hearts to "do by nature things required by the law" (Rom. 2:14) and that "the law is holy, and the commandment is holy, righteous and good" (Rom. 7:12) leave no doubt that obedience to God's Law enriches people's lives, just as disregard for God's Law destroys life. Nevertheless, since "there is no one righteous, not even one" (Rom. 3:10) and since "no one will be declared righteous in [God's] sight by observing the law" (Rom. 3:20), outwardly keeping the Law results in blessings and positive results that are not spiritual and eternal, but earthly and temporal. Our good God who caringly looks after His creation "causes his sun to rise on the evil and the good, and sends rain on the righteous and the unrighteous" (Matt. 5:45). He preserves "both man and beast." (Ps. 36:6). Of Him the Psalmist writes, "You open your hand and satisfy the desires of every living thing" (Ps. 145:16). He chooses to bless outward compliance with His will with temporal, positive benefits.

The Bible and the Scripture-based writings of Dr. Martin Luther aid us in further understanding how God blesses the lives of people, including those who are not yet Christians. In his gospel account John tells us about Jesus' conversation with the Roman governor Pontius Pilate, in which Jesus revealed that God rules in two ways. When the governor asked Jesus if He were a king, Jesus answered, "My kingdom is not of this world. If it were, my servants would fight to prevent my arrest by the Jews. But now my kingdom is from another place"

(John 18:36). God provides two kinds of government, one secular (temporal), and the other spiritual.

Drawing on the teachings of Scripture, Dr. Martin Luther wrote extensively about these two ways that God rules. God rules in the spiritual realm through His saving revelation of Jesus Christ, providing people with spiritual and eternal benefits. Dr. Luther sometimes called this God's rule with His right hand. In turn, Luther observed that God also rules in the secular realm with His left hand, endowing people with earthly or temporal blessings.

God's left-hand rule includes civil or political government. Contrasting the blessings of civil government with God's spiritual rule, Luther had this to say:

> God has ordained two governments: the spiritual, by which the Holy Spirit produces Christians and righteous people under Christ; and the temporal, which restrains the un-Christian and wicked so that no thanks to them they are obliged to keep still and to maintain an outward peace . . .
>
> One must carefully distinguish between these two governments. Both must be permitted to remain: the one to produce righteousness, the other to bring about external peace and prevent evil deeds.[8]

Elsewhere, Dr. Luther wrote about God's temporal blessings upon people, focusing, not on civil government, but rather on blessings and benefits in general. In one writing he spoke at some length about the variety of God's temporal blessings:

> God has a double blessing, a physical one for this life and a spiritual one for eternal life. Hence we say that it is a blessing to have riches, children, etc., but only at its own level, namely, for this present life . . . God dispenses these gifts of His freely in the world to both good and bad, just as "He makes His sun rise on the evil and on the good, and sends rain on the just and on the unjust" (Matt. 5:45), for He is generous to everyone . . . Those who have only these physical blessings are not on that account the sons of God,

spiritually blessed in the sight of God, as Abraham was. They are under a curse, as Paul says: "All who rely on works of the Law are under a curse."[9]

Martin Luther's study of the Bible taught him that the secular government includes more than political structures and authorities. As Paul Althaus wrote in his book *The Ethics of Martin Luther.*

> It [secular government] includes everything that contributes to the preservation of this earthly life, especially marriage and family, the entire household, as well as property, business, and all stations and vocations which God has instituted.[10]

The doctrine of God's rule in the secular realm explains how God gives temporal blessings to all people in many ways.

Three Teachings Applied to the Twelve Steps

Three Bible teachings provide us resources to meet the challenge of formulating a Christian response to the Twelve Steps. The first is the Bible's instruction about the natural knowledge of God, that, independent of His Scriptural revelation, we are able to know some things about God and His will for us. The second teaching regards all people's ability to do outwardly good works that benefit themselves and others. The third word of instruction is that God rules in both the secular and spiritual realms. He rules in the secular realm, giving physical benefits here and now; He rules in the spiritual realm, giving spiritual and eternal gifts.

Applied to the Twelve Steps, these teachings persuasively show that the steps can indeed provide temporal good to those who practice them. The significance of this conclusion we shall explore more fully in the next chapter.

---

1. Theodore Tappert, ed. and trans., *The Book of Concord* (Philadelphia: Fortress Press, 1959), 108.

2. Ibid., 521.

3. Francis Pieper, *Christian Dogmatics,* vol. 1 (St. Louis: Concordia Publishing House, 1950), 371.

4. Edward W. A. Koehler, *A Short Exposition of Dr. Martin Luther's Small Catechism Edited by the Evangelical Lutheran Synod of Missouri, Ohio, and other States with ADDITIONAL NOTES for Students, Teachers, and Pastors* (Fort Wayne: Concordia Theological Seminary Press, 1981), 38–39.

5. Edmund Schlink, *Theology of the Lutheran Confessions* (Philadelphia: Muhlenberg, 1961), 75.

6. Tappert, *Book of Concord,* 146.

7. Ibid, 224–26.

8. Martin Luther, "Temporal Authority To What Extent It Should Be Obeyed," in *Luther's Works* (American Edition), ed. Helmut T. Lehmann, vol. 45: *The Christian in Society II,* ed. Walter I. Brandt (Philadelphia: Muhlenberg Press, 1962), 91–92.

9. Martin Luther, "Lectures on Galatians 1535," in *Luther's Works* (American Edition), ed. Jaroslav Pelikan and Walter A. Hansen, vol. 26: *Lectures on Galatians 1535,* trans. Jaroslav Pelikan (St. Louis: Concordia Publishing House, 1963), 251.

10. Paul Althaus, *The Ethics of Martin Luther,* trans. Robert C. Schultz (Philadelphia: Fortress Press, 1972), 47.

Chapter 7

Biblical Conclusions about the Twelve Steps

God Uses the Twelve Steps

Persuasive biblical reasons compel us to believe that God uses the Twelve Step Program to empower people to recover from addictions and thus improve their physical and emotional health. As the First Article of the Apostles' Creed affirms, God is merciful and good to all people of His creation. He provides not only for Christian people, but also for those who are not yet in a saving relationship with Him through faith in Christ. God makes it possible for everyone to have knowledge of Him, even though that knowledge is limited and too often distorted by its users. Furthermore, He gives people the ability to use their knowledge of God for their own physical and social welfare and that of others.

The benefits of the Twelve Steps come to people through their natural knowledge of God and their capacity to respond with outward good works. God works in the secular sphere as well as in the spiritual, rules with His left hand as well as His right. Lutheranism's Augsburg Confession quotes St. Augustine with approval for saying that no acts of civil righteousness exist without God, but "all things are from him and through him."[1] John Meyer summarizes Martin Luther's thoughts on this matter, as follows:

> Luther drew a sharp line of demarcation between the two realms. The spiritual realm is without external power. Its power is exercised by God Himself through the Word and the preaching office. The secular realm is subject to human reason, and its authority is exercised by men who have the power to enforce

laws, etc. It is God Himself who is active in both realms, and thus they are united. In the spiritual sphere God works through the Gospel to save men, and in the secular He works through the Law and impels men to live in a certain way, to do good and avoid evil.[2]

As part of God's goodness in the secular realm, the Twelve Steps surely bestow health-giving influences as His very own benefits. Through the steps God offers a share of the "daily bread" of "peace and health" Luther mentions in his explanation of the Fourth Petition of the Lord's Prayer.[3]

Our biblical study shapes our view of the steps. We are able to argue that by God's goodness the surrender to a Higher Power that Step Three calls for takes place because people employ both their natural knowledge of God and their free will to do outwardly good works. Because God cares for people in the secular realm, their surrender generates a psychological or personality change that produces recovery. If we were to explain recovery in biblical language, we might say that doing Step Three produces a kind of psychological conversion experience.

The Commission on Organizations of The Lutheran Church—Missouri Synod makes a similar observation. Without offering a theological explanation for its conclusion as our study does, the Commission affirms that, "The 'spiritual awakening' to which frequent reference is made in A.A. literature does not refer to 'conversion' but to a personality change sufficient to bring about recovery from alcoholism, however that change may take place."[4] These words are reminiscent of a comment Herbert Spencer made in *Alcoholics Anonymous*. He observed that "the terms 'spiritual experience' and 'spiritual awakening' are used many times in this book which, upon careful reading, shows that the personality change sufficient to bring about recovery from alcoholism has manifested itself among us in many different forms."[5]

God's Word enables us to say positive things about the Twelve Steps. In shaping a view of the steps faithful to Scripture, however, our study does not allow us to say only favorable things about the Twelve Steps. We need to say more.

Incompleteness of the Steps

Even though we view the steps as God's good gift for people's temporal welfare, Bill W.'s Twelve Step Spiritual Program of Recovery is, as is any expression of natural theology, seriously lacking when assessed on the basis of God's revelation in Jesus Christ and in the Sacred Scriptures. From a Christian perspective the steps are both seriously incomplete and potentially misleading. They do not testify to the God who has revealed Himself in His Son and in the Bible. They do not introduce the practitioner to the saving work of God's Son, Jesus Christ, who lived among us in perfect obedience to God and died on a cross to make good for disobedient lives. They do not proclaim that people are restored to God's presence and power through faith, solely through faith, in Jesus Christ.

Since the Twelve Step Program is regarded as a *spiritual* program and one that speaks of God in various ways, the truly grave danger of the program is that those who practice the steps might readily view the steps as giving more than a blessing of God for physical health. They might look upon the steps as affording the fullness of God's spiritual gifts which He gives only in the redeeming work of Jesus Christ—the forgiveness of sins, the life-changing power of the Holy Spirit, and an unending life with God.

A sample of official A.A. language that might mislead the Twelve Step practitioner are Bill W.'s comments in the Big Book chapter entitled, "There Is a Solution." There, as my added emphases point out, he wrote that the steps give benefits associated with the Christian faith.

> *There is a solution.* Almost none of us liked the self-searching, the leveling of our pride, the confession of shortcomings which the process requires for its successful consummation. But we saw that it really worked in others, and we had come to believe in the hopelessness and futility of life as we had been living it. When, therefore, we were approached by those in

71

whom the problem had been solved, there was nothing left for us but to pick up *the simple kit of spiritual tools* laid at our feet. *We have found much of heaven and we have been rocketed into a fourth dimension of existence of which we had not ever dreamed.*

The great fact is just this, and nothing less: that *we have had deep and effective spiritual experiences which have revolutionized our whole attitude toward life, toward our fellows and toward God's universe.* The central fact of our lives today is the absolute certainty that *our Creator has entered into our hearts and lives in a way which is indeed miraculous. He has commenced to accomplish those things for us which we could never do by ourselves.*[6]

In another place Bill wrote, "All of us, whatever our race, creed, or color are children of a loving Creator with whom we may form a relationship upon simple and understandable terms as soon as we are willing and honest enough to try."[7]

If perhaps Bill's words could be understood in the sense of God's secular rule, they might possibly be acceptably interpreted, but, taken as they read, they are perilously misleading with regard to God's saving plans, provisions, and activities associated only with His saving spiritual rule.

Some of Bill's statements may seem ambiguous, but others do not readily offer room for a possible variety of interpretations. For example, the Big Book includes disclaimers that the Twelve Step Program is in any way religious, but, in introducing his solution to alcoholism in his first volume, Bill stated, "Of necessity there will have to be discussion of matters medical, psychiatric, social, and religious."[8] Even more weighty, both implicit and explicit in Bill W.'s Twelve Step commentary is the belief that God forgives the sins of anyone who asks Him for forgiveness. For example, an explicit comment regarding forgiveness appears in Bill W.'s advice in his Eleventh Step discussion of prayer. There he wrote, "We ask God's forgiveness and inquire what corrective measures should be taken."[9] These words, we recall, refer to the Higher Power or God *as we understood Him.*

Bill's comments about religious matters, most notably his words about seeking forgiveness, are especially troublesome and misleading. There is only one way to obtain the forgiveness of sins as, faithful to Scripture, Article IV of the Augsburg Confession declares:

> We cannot obtain forgiveness of sin and righteousness before God by our own merits, works, or satisfactions, but that we receive forgiveness of sin and become righteous before God by grace, for Christ's sake through faith, when we believe that Christ suffered for us and that for his sake our sin is forgiven and righteousness and eternal life are given to us. For God will regard and reckon this faith as righteousness, as Paul says in Romans 3:21–26 and 4:5.[10]

A Limited Blessing

Because the Twelve Step Program can mediate the gift of temporal well-being, it is truly a good blessing of God. From the perspective of the Bible, however, the Twelve Steps are incomplete because they do not present God as the One who has revealed Himself in Jesus Christ and who accepts and totally transforms people who believe in Christ. Even more serious, the Twelve Step Program presents God as a God who forgives sin apart from personal faith in Jesus Christ as Savior. This is the realistic biblical assessment the steps challenge us to provide. It affirms the benefits of the steps and, at the same time, straightforwardly expresses serious Christian concerns and cautions. In turn, this assessment prepares us to discuss the opportunity that the Twelve Step Program sets before the Church.

---

1. Theodore Tappert, ed. and trans., *The Book of Concord,* (Philadelphia: Fortress Press, 1959), 39–40.
2. John R. Meyer, "Luther's Doctrine of the Two Kingdoms," *Andrews University Seminary Studies* 12 (January 1974):9.
3. Tappert, *Book of Concord,* 347.
4. The Lutheran Church—Missouri Synod Commission on Organizations, "Alcoholics Anonymous," 1970. (Mimeographed)

5. [William G. Wilson et al.], *Alcoholics Anonymous,* rev. 2d ed. (New York: Alcoholics Anonymous Publishing, Inc., 1955), 569.

6. Ibid., 25.

7. Ibid., 28.

8. Ibid., 19.

9. Ibid., 86.

10. Ibid., *Book of Concord,* 30.

Part 3

The Twelve Steps— Opportunity for the Church

Chapter 8

The Opportunity for Sharing the Gospel with Twelve Step Practitioners

Extraordinary Opportunities for Sharing

In the last two chapters we responded to the challenge to discover and use scriptural resources to hammer out a biblical view of the Twelve Steps. Now, on the basis of our conclusions, we discover that the steps afford the church extraordinary opportunities. The first of these is the opportunity to reach out with the Gospel to people who practice the Twelve Steps, Christians and non-Christians alike.

As we have learned, Twelve Step practitioners through a variety of mutual-help groups receive and give support as they use the steps to deal with addictive behaviors. These groups comprise literally millions of hurting people who acknowledge their need for spiritual help to live liberated and serene lives. They include addicted or dependent persons and also coaddicted or codependent persons, that is, individuals who live in a close relationship with addicts and are adversely affected by their addictive lifestyle.

Professing Christians as well as non-Christians belong to Twelve Step groups. Since the members of these groups understand God and the spiritual life in many different ways, recovering Christians in these groups need the encouragement and support of one another and other Christians to interpret and use the Twelve Steps in Christian ways. In turn, Christians both inside and outside Twelve Step groups have opportunities to share with non-Christians in Twelve Step groups how to understand and practice the Twelve Steps within the context of the Christian faith.

Sharing Among Twelve Step Christians

In response to a letter of inquiry from Dr. Sam Shoemaker, Bill Wilson once suggested that "a group of A.A.'s" and "a group of A.A.'s in the church" might find it helpful to form small groups for the purpose of Bible study and mutual Christian support. He commented that "anyone" might be invited to join them. His enthusiasm for this development is unmistakable: "There is no reason why a group of A.A.'s shouldn't get together for Bible study; no reason at all why a group of A.A.'s in a church should not associate themselves into a sort of spiritual kindergarten fellowship, in which anyone might be invited. As a matter of fact, I am anxious to see this sort of thing tried."[1]

Bible study and mutual care among Christians associated with Twelve Step groups, as well as those in other kinds of groups, give us Christians the opportunity to help each other recognize that the only Higher Power that can save and change lives is God, the Father of our Lord Jesus Christ. Lest we forget, we remind each other that only those persons who are right with God through faith in Jesus and, as a result, have the Holy Spirit's life-transforming power, can work the steps for the fullness of God's blessing. We continually assure one another of God's forgiveness and constant love in Jesus. We speak of that love to encourage one another and, of even greater importance, to make available to one another the Gospel, which is God's power enabling us to work the steps in God-pleasing ways. St. Paul writes, "Speaking the truth in love, we will in all things grow up into him who is the Head, that is, Christ" (Eph. 4:15).

Sharing with Non-Christians

Just as Christians need to care for one another, so we also need to give Christian care to non-Christians who work the Twelve Step Program. As we have said, we desire to lead non-Christians to a Christian understanding and use of the steps so that they, too, can enjoy the fullness of God's rich spiritual blessings for recovery.

The ministry of the apostle Paul in the city of Athens (Acts 17:16–34) gives us an example of how to reach out to non-Christians. At the meeting of the Areopagus, commenting about one of their many altars, the altar dedicated to "AN UNKNOWN GOD," Paul said to the citizens of Athens, "Now what you worship as something unknown I am going to proclaim to you" (Acts 17:23). Then he spoke to his hearers about the one true God. He preached about God's creative work, His care for the people of His creation, His call for repentance, and the appointed Judge whom God had raised from the dead.

The parallel is apparent. In Twelve Step groups many persons are seeking both for spiritual resources for their lives and for the identity of the too often "Unknown God." These people have suffered greatly from addictions. They have deeply and painfully felt the effects of living in ways that are contrary to God's Law. Through their pain God Himself has acted to prepare them to hear the Gospel. According to St. Paul, these people are seeking God and reaching out for Him. (Acts 17:27). In the words of Jesus, they are "fields ripe for the harvest":

> "My food," said Jesus, "is to do the will of him who sent me and to finish his work. Do you not say, 'Four months more and then the harvest'? I tell you, open your eyes and look at the fields! They are ripe for harvest. Even now the reaper draws his wages, even now he harvests the crop for eternal life, so that the sower and the reaper may be glad together" (John 4:34–36).

Shoemaker's Advice

Like the apostle Paul, Dr. Sam Shoemaker's example incites us to commend dependent and codependent Twelve Step workers to Christ and His church. On several occasions Dr. Shoemaker commented that A.A. is "as a precursor to the Church, . . . what St. Paul called the Law, a tutor to get us ready for the church." As a precursor, Shoemaker said, "I think

AA stands second to none."[2] In another place he expressed much the same thought, adding that "Alcoholics Anonymous are [sic] giving a great lead in witness to spiritual truth and power, and are often what St. Paul said the law was, a 'tutor' to bring people to *Christ*"[3] as well as to the church [emphasis added].

Speaking the Truth in Love

Just as important as what we say to dependent and codependent persons is the way we say it. The very nature of addictive disorders persuades us to follow earnestly St. Paul's counsel always to speak the truth in love (Eph. 4:15). He encourages us to speak about God's will and love with great care and concern for others. Paul's words are so important to hear and heed because dependents and codependents, like so many of us, tend to be defensive when confronted.

Several factors foster defensiveness in dependent and codependent individuals. We need to be aware of them as we shape the way we speak.

First, addiction to a substance, behavior, or person causes dependent people to put the substance, behavior, or person at the center of their lives, becoming more important even than God. In fact, the substance, behavior, or person ultimately becomes their "god," and people readily resist having anything taken away from them that they consider essential for their lives. Misled into distorted and dishonest thinking by their addiction, they fail to recognize and acknowledge their true spiritual problems and true spiritual solutions.

Second, many addicted persons have had unhappy experiences with Christians, including professional church workers. They believe these people have devalued them, judged them harshly, or given them simplistic and unhelpful advice. They frequently feel the need to defend themselves from people of the church, especially its leaders.

Third, many addicted persons are not only angry with Christian leaders and the church, but they are also angry with

God Himself because He has not helped them when and how they wanted Him to help.

Finally, those affected by addictions often have moments of deep pain in their lives. When these times come, they feel so guilty before God that they look for relief by denying the truth about their sinful condition. They cannot long endure facing the truth about their addictive lifestyle.

To be sure, "speaking the truth in love" is extremely important as we try to extend Christian caring to dependent and codependent persons. By faithfully speaking in love the message of God's good will and His gracious forgiveness, we sacrifice neither truth nor love. Instead, we show respect to people and help them nondefensively to hear and think about God's good news. We want them to hear it in ways that enable the Holy Spirit of God to work faith, renew their minds, and change their behavior. We recognize, as St. Paul teaches, that faith comes from *hearing* the word of Christ (Rom. 10:17) and not just from talking, especially talking that does not facilitate hearing.

Furthermore, speaking the truth in love involves beginning with people where they are in their relationship with God. Our example is Jesus' conversation with the woman at Jacob's well (John 4:1–42). There He displayed understanding of the woman's thoughts, beliefs, and style of living. He did not approve of her values or actions, but this did not keep Him from empathically caring for her. Truthfully and lovingly the Lord talked with her where He had discovered her to be. His words felt right to the woman in terms of her experience.

When, like Jesus, we address people beginning with their felt needs, we readily engage their hearing. By sharing the story of our own relationship with Jesus Christ, including our own needs, struggles, beliefs, blessings, and hopes, in ways that have meaning for our hearers, we gain their attention.

While we make judgments (in order to be helpful) about people's beliefs and behaviors, we seek to be nonjudgmental of them as persons. We endeavor to give them respect as created by God and redeemed by Jesus Christ. In this way we foster a relationship of openness and trust.

People's disagreements with us do not give us right or reason to treat them unkindly. Rather, dialoging with them, we discover points of contact enabling us to share Christ's love and message with great care and concern. Thus God's faith-generating, saving, and life-changing power, the Gospel, has its best opportunity to endow them with a faith relationship with Him through Jesus Christ.

Nothing could be more important for recovery than faith in Christ, because in the relationship with Christ God gives addiction-affected persons His best spiritual resources. He bestows His rich gifts that flow from all that Jesus won for us by His life, death, and resurrection: the forgiveness of sins, life now and eternally, and salvation here and hereafter.

Some people have a lot of difficulty in their "seeking and reaching out" (Acts 17:27) for God. Though they say they seek and reach out for Him, they do not find Him. All the more, then, we need patiently and untiringly to share our Christian experience of God's will and God's love.

Is there anything else we can do? The Formula of Concord offers us a suggestion. It states that "the person who is not yet converted to God and regenerated can hear and read this Word externally because, as stated above, even after the Fall man still has something of a free will in these external matters, so that he can go to church, listen to the sermon, or not listen to it."[4] As we share our own faith experiences with searching people, we will do well to encourage them to place themselves under the power of God by hearing and reading His Word, by living in the Christian community, and by listening to the preaching of sermons at worship.

Of course, Christians who are recovering from dependency and codependency by practicing the Twelve Steps have "built-in" opportunities to commend the Gospel to others seeking spiritual help for recovery. Their association with Twelve Step groups puts them in touch with many people who require Christian care and the assistance of God. They can readily build trusting and caring relationships with these people.

Such opportunities, however, are not limited to Christians in recovery. At what are called "open meetings" of mutual-help groups, each and every Christian can meet recovering persons to whom we can give friendship and care. In turn, we can expect our lives to be enriched in many ways by our association with those who practice the Twelve Steps. Many of them are models of honesty, openness, trust, and caring for others.

Fifth Step Work

As another way to reach out to Twelve Step practitioners, all of us concerned Christians, especially professional church workers, can make ourselves available to assist recovering persons with Fifth Step work. Those who take the Fifth Step need a trustworthy and understanding person to whom they might admit the exact nature of their wrongs. People who are Christians or were brought up Christian often look for a Christian, frequently a pastor, with whom to make their Fifth Step confession. Surely, God calls on all of us who bear the name of Christ, pastors and people of God alike, both within and without Twelve Step groups, to make use of every opportunity to share the story of the Christian faith and life and to do so with empathy, sensitivity, and great care.

God at Work

God appears to be working a great work in our day. Millions of people are suffering from addictions to alcohol, drugs, or other substances or behaviors. Additional millions suffer because of the addictions of family members or friends. Many of them are seeking recovery by practicing the Twelve Steps. Undoubtedly, through people's use of the Twelve Step Program God is providing opportunities for caring Christians to communicate by words and actions the Gospel of God's love to those searching for God and His spiritual gifts. Our ministry among these suffering people is surely God's way of overcoming the evils of addiction. Even more awesome, through the dedicated service of His people God makes the evils of addiction serve His saving purposes as people recover by His help in Jesus, His Son. We and all God's people are more than conquerors over evil through Him who loved us (Rom. 8:35–37).

Jesus' parable of the lost son and the forgiving father clearly shows us God's purposes and our part in His plan. Addictions lead people into a "distant country" of severe pain that purposes to lead them back to the Father. On our part, we have the privilege of introducing them to the compassionate Father who, for the sake of His Son Jesus, forgives, comforts, and gives hope and life-transforming power to those who trust in Him. Restored to the Father, those who were dead are alive again; those who were lost are found (Luke 15:11–32). God calls us not to neglect the great opportunity He sets before us but to make the most of it.

---

1. William G. Wilson to Samuel M. Shoemaker, 2 May 1958, Shoemaker Papers, Record Group 101-21-6, Episcopal Church Archives, Austin Texas.

2. Samuel M. Shoemaker, "The Spiritual Part of AA," *Grapevine* 17 (November 1960), 13.

3. Samuel M. Shoemaker, *Revive Thy Church Beginning with Me* (New York: Harper & Bros., Publishers, 1948), 72.

4. Theodore Tappert, ed. and trans., *The Book of Concord* (Philadelphia: Fortress Press, 1959), 531.

Chapter 9

The Opportunity for Enriching Christian Growth

Two Possibilities for Growth

The practice of the Twelve Steps by people associated with various mutual-help groups suggests two opportunities for the church. In the last chapter, we discussed at length the first opportunity: to share the Gospel in words and actions with those who practice the Twelve Steps.

The second opportunity the Twelve Steps put before the church concerns Christian growth. The Twelve Step Program provides the church a basis of comparison by which to review, evaluate, and enrich its own process of Christian growth. The Twelve Steps suggest two possibilities for promoting Christian growth.

First, the program encourages Christians to practice intentional, goal-directed sanctification (Christian growth). It offers, for those who choose to use them, the opportunity to revise the steps for Christian purposes.

Second, the Twelve Step Program underscores and emphasizes the traditional Christian practice of facilitating Christian growth by providing mutual care in small groups.

Practicing Intentional Sanctification

What is intentional, goal-directed sanctification or Christian growth, and why is it important to practice it?

To answer these questions, let us first recall something we have already learned: Twelve Step practitioners *intentionally use* the Twelve Steps to achieve *a particular goal*. Their goal is to recover from addiction or coaddiction. Having both a process and a goal can facilitate Christian growth.

Actually, Twelve Step practice simply reminds us to affirm something the Bible teaches. The Bible clearly instructs Christians to use the power of the Holy Spirit to live the Christian life in an intentional and goal-directed way.

This is what the Bible has to say about Christian living and growing: When God gives us faith to believe in Jesus as our Savior from sin and death and forgives our sins for Jesus' sake, God at the same time begins to transform our lives. He makes us able to will and act according to His good purpose (2 Cor. 5: 15–19; Eph. 2:8–10; Phil. 2:13). We say that God sanctifies us. Having *pronounced* us holy for Jesus' sake, God then begins to *make* us holy in the way we live.

This is what we are like as Christians: God in grace forgives us our sins and makes us spiritually alive. In God's eyes we are holy, yet, at the same time, we continue to sin because facets of our being—our thinking, feeling, and doing—are not yet fully under the influence of the Spirit of God. God's power at work in us enables us, however, to struggle against sin and evil and to achieve good. We desire to grow as Christians because God Himself inspires and empowers us to struggle against doing evil, to endeavor to do good, and to experience newness of life in Christ.

To equip us to overcome the sins that assault us and to achieve Christian faith and life goals, God employs the same Gospel message of His love and forgiveness that He first used to bring us to faith (1 Peter 1:23–2:3; Eph. 4:15). In love for us God outfits us to identify a problem of faith or life that needs attention, choose the faith or life goal(s) we want to attain, and energetically use God's own power, the Gospel, to overcome our targeted sin(s) and accomplish our goal(s).

St. Paul clearly teaches that God gives us the desire and ability to grow intentionally and successfully as Christians. Because we live under God's grace, Paul says, we are dead to sin and alive to God. We are able to assert ourselves; we can "offer ourselves to God." In his letter to the Romans he writes:

> Count yourselves dead to sin but alive to God in Christ Jesus. Therefore *do not let* sin reign in your mortal body so that you obey its evil desires. *Do not offer* the parts of your body to sin, as instruments of wickedness, but *rather offer yourselves* to God, as those who have been brought from death to life; and *offer the parts of your body* to him as instruments of righteousness. For sin shall not be your master, because you are not under law, but under grace [emphases added] . . .
>
> I put this in human terms because you are weak in your natural selves. Just as you used to offer the parts of your body in slavery to impurity and to ever-increasing wickedness, so now offer them in slavery to righteousness leading to holiness (Rom. 6:11–14, 19).

Truly, "we are God's workmanship, created in Christ Jesus to do good works, which God prepared in advance for us to do" (Eph. 2:10).

Often we Christians fail to understand that, even though we can do absolutely nothing to establish a right relationship with God, we are able, once we are in a right relationship with God, intentionally, energetically, and purposefully to make use of the power of the Holy Spirit to do God's will. This is what God wants. Consequently St. Paul writes:

> Therefore, I urge you, brothers, in view of God's mercy, to *offer your bodies* as living sacrifices, holy and pleasing to God—this is your spiritual act of worship. *Do not conform* any longer to the pattern of this world, but be transformed by the renewing of your mind. Then you will be able to test and approve what God's will is—his good, pleasing and perfect will [emphases added] (Rom. 12:1–2).

In his letters, however, Paul not only speaks of sanctification as intentional but also as goal-directed. For example, in his letter to the Ephesians the apostle illustrates the use of goals in the practice of intentional sanctification. He tells his hearers about specific sins to overcome and particular goals to achieve. Then, he speaks the Gospel to empower his hearers to overcome their sins and grow toward definite Christian goals. The apostle Paul writes:

> So I tell you this, and insist on it in the Lord, that you must no longer live as the Gentiles do, in the futility of their thinking . . .
>
> You, however, did not come to know Christ that way. Surely you heard of him and were taught in him in accordance with the truth that is in Jesus. You were taught, with regard to your former way of life, to put off your old self, which is being corrupted by its deceitful desires; to be made new in the attitude of your minds; and to put on the new self, created to be like God in true righteousness and holiness.
>
> Therefore each of you must put off falsehood and speak truthfully to his neighbor, for we are all members of one body. "In your anger do not sin": Do not let the sun go down while you are still angry, and do not give the devil a foothold. He who has been stealing must steal no longer, but must work, doing something useful with his own hands, that he may have something to share with those in need.
>
> Do not let any unwholesome talk come out of your mouths, but only what is helpful for building others up according to their needs, that it may benefit those who listen. And do not grieve the Holy Spirit of God, with whom you were sealed for the day of redemption. Get rid of all bitterness, rage and anger, brawling and slander, along with every form of malice. Be kind and compassionate to one another, forgiving each other, just as in Christ God forgave you.
>
> Be imitators of God, therefore, as dearly loved children and live a life of love, just as Christ loved us and gave himself up for us as a fragrant offering and sacrifice to God (Eph. 4:17, 20–5:2).

Obviously, God does not want us to follow our natural tendencies, sitting around waiting for Him magically and mysteriously to force a change of life on us. God simply does not work that way. Rather, He wants us, with the deliberate and strong intent of minds renewed by the Holy Spirit, to use the energy generated in us by the Holy Spirit to work whole-heartedly to overcome the sin in our lives and grow in Christian living by the power of the Gospel. The Formula of Concord offers us these encouraging words:

> As soon as the Holy Spirit has initiated his work of regeneration and renewal in us through the Word and the holy sacraments, *it is certain that we can and must cooperate by the power of the Holy Spirit, even though we still do so in great weakness.* Such cooperation does not proceed from our carnal and natural powers, but from the new powers and gifts which the Holy Spirit has begun in us in conversion, as St. Paul expressly and earnestly reminds us, "Working together with him, then we entreat you not to accept the grace of God in vain [emphasis added]."[1]

A Christian Version of Twelve Steps

As suggested earlier in this chapter, the Twelve Steps appear to hold promise for those committed to the practice of intentional, goal-directed spiritual growth. This means the steps offer assistance to a Christian who wants to work with a specific problem, overcome that problem, achieve a specific goal, and thus grow as a Christian.

What follows is a Christian adaptation of the Twelve Steps that help Christians accomplish purposeful growth. Again, we emphasize that the steps can help Christians further their Christian growth, but they cannot help anyone get right with God.

Given only as a suggestion, the proposed revision reads:

Because God has endowed us with repentance to know and confess our sins and to trust in Jesus Christ for the forgiveness of sins and the renewal of life, which God has so graciously given us, we are able to:

1. Admit that we are sinners as well as forgiven and renewed people. We daily sin much and often find ourselves powerless over facets of our lives that are not under the control

of the Holy Spirit and that dishonor God and cause hurt to ourselves and to others.

2. Believe that God can and does daily forgive our sins for Jesus' sake and liberate and renew our lives through the work of the Holy Spirit.

3. Under the Holy Spirit's power, make a decision daily, especially with reference to specific concerns, to turn our will and our lives over to the care of God and His recreating power and to make fuller use of His gift of the Holy Spirit for changing facets of our lives identified as needing transformation.

4. Make a searching and fearless inventory of our sinfulness and sinful actions that need immediate attention.

5. Admit to ourselves, to God, and at least one other Christian the exact nature of our sins, and consider making private confession before the pastor and receiving holy absolution from God through the pastor.

6. Be ready to have God remove our sinful behavior.

7. Humbly ask Him to remove our sinful behavior.

8. Make a list of all persons we have harmed, and be willing to make amends to them all.

9. Make direct amends to such people wherever possible, except when to do so would injure them or others.

10. Continue day by day to do what we are committed to do and have been doing: take a personal inventory and when we sin, promptly admit our sin, receive God's forgiveness and life-renewing power, and respond in responsible Christian ways.

11. Through the use of God's Word and the Lord's Supper, seek to enrich our relationship with God. By the use of God's Word and prayer, seek a clearer understanding of God's will and the ability to carry it out.

12. Carry the message of the saving and liberating Gospel of Jesus Christ to people in need of God's life-transforming resources to deal with a variety of concerns and, finally, to seek to express our growing Christian maturity in all aspects of life.

An Illustration of Christian Use

Perhaps an illustration can show how to use the adapted Twelve Steps for intentional, goal-directed Christian growth. Think of yourself as a codependent person. You often feel inferior to others and devalue yourself. Out of anger and depression, you try to feel and appear better by controlling other people, taking advantage of them, and "putting them down." When you cannot control others, you feel even worse about yourself. This, of course, is not the way you want to be. In fact, you sense that as a Christian you have good reasons to value yourself much more than you do. Your goal is to value yourself as God values you because of Christ.

What can you do to achieve your goal? In brief, admit that of yourself you are powerless over your attitude of poor self-esteem. Recognize that your heavenly Father wants you to know your true worth as His child. He stands ready to forgive your faulty perceptions and actions and to change your attitudes and behavior. Therefore, intentionally turn yourself over to the care of God, confessing your sins of belittling yourself and hurting others. Ask God to take away your low self-esteem and resulting hurtful behaviors. Recall from His Word the forgiving love He has for you in Christ. Be assured that Christ has paid for your sins and that God forgives also your sins of self-depreciation and the misuse of others and that He values you highly as His very own possession. Ask another person, perhaps your pastor, to hear your confession and announce to you God's forgiveness for the particular sins with which you are dealing.

As you rely on God for help, His full forgiveness for Jesus' sake will truly comfort you and empower you toward overcoming your sins of thinking little of yourself and of treating others badly in an attempt to feel better. By the Gospel God will enable you more closely to reach your goals to have healthier esteem for yourself and others and to struggle successfully more often than not against the temptation to devalue and abuse yourself and others. You may take one step forward toward your goal, or several, only to fall back; but you continue to practice the steps. Christian growth is a lifelong process.

As God's love reaches deeply into your life, you may want to make amends to people you have hurt. God Himself enables such amends-making and through it heals damaged relationships and blesses us with a sense of integrity.

This is simply one illustration of ways a Christian understanding of the Twelve Steps might aid us in practicing intentional, goal directed Christian growth. We can apply these same principles to the misuse of drugs, food, money, sex, and power. The Christianized steps can help us deal with any sins that readily entangle us: bad temper, impatience, jealously, hatred, or selfish ambition. They can assist us in fulfilling the instruction of the writer to the Hebrews:

> Let us throw off everything that hinders and *the sin that so easily entangles* [emphasis added], and let us run with perseverance the race marked out for us. Let us fix our eyes on Jesus, the author and perfecter of our faith, who for the joy set before him endured the cross, scorning its shame, and sat down at the right hand of the throne of God (Heb. 12:1–2).

As we Christianize the Twelve Steps and use them for the purpose of Christian growth, it is important to recognize that Scripture teachings are reflected in the Twelve Steps. We readily recall that Scripture teaches us we are powerless over sin that tightly controls us (Rom. 3:9–20; Eph. 2:1–3) and that only God can rescue us from sin and all its evils (Rom. 3:21–28; Rom. 8:1–17; Gal. 3:10–14). Turning to God in faith by His power at work in us through His Word and Holy Baptism, we are restored to a right relationship with Him and set free to strive to live according to the teachings of Jesus, who died for us and rose again (Eph. 2:1–10; 2 Cor. 5:14–21; Rom. 6:1–14; Rom. 10:1–17; Titus 3:3–8). Because of His undeserved love toward us, God enables us continually to recognize and confess our sins, to ask Him to remove our sins, to be caring about those we have hurt and harmed, and to want to amend our sinful lives (Titus 2:11–14; Ps. 32; Ps. 51; 1 John 1:5–10;

James 5:16; Gal. 5:22–23; Luke 3:7–14; Luke 19:1–10; Heb. 12:1–2). God empowers us to be Christians who continually draw closer to Him by prayerfully living among His people under the life-changing power of His Word and Holy Supper (Acts 2:42–47; 2 Tim. 3:15–17; 1 Peter 1:23–2:3; 1 Cor. 10:16–17). He gives us the deep desire to speak of His love to others and tell how His forgiving goodness transforms lives (1 Peter 2:9–12; John 4:4–30, 39–42; Acts 1:1–11).

A Christian expression of the Twelve Steps certainly reminds us that God provides all Christians the capability to live the new life in Christ by setting intentional goals. In his *Small Catechism* Martin Luther outlined the intentional Christian life of every baptized believer:

> It [baptism] indicates that the Old Adam in us should by daily contrition and repentance be drowned and die with all sins and evil desires, and that a new man should daily emerge and arise to live before God in righteousness and purity forever.[2]

Christian Mutual-Help Groups

Now we come to a second way the Twelve Steps can further Christian growth. People usually practice the Twelve Steps in association with mutual-help groups. This practice underscores and emphasizes a practice that is very much a part of the church's history and tradition, though in some places the church needs to value it more highly and use it more fully.

Since the days of the apostles, Christians cared for one another's faith and life in Christ, not only in large worship assemblies, but also in small groups dedicated to more personal mutual care. Small group gatherings permit us to deal with specific concerns and give and receive care and encouragement in open and trusting relationships. Small groups provide a forum for aiding and supporting one another in choosing and carrying forward the work of intentional, goal directed sanctification.

Dr. Sam Shoemaker possessed a deep conviction that fellowship is fostered in the church not only in worship assembles but also by the formation of small groups. He believed the church could learn from A.A. fellowships that "we need to supplement what we do now by the establishment of informal companies where people who are spiritually seeking can see how faith takes hold in other lives."

In his book *How You Can Help Other People* Shoemaker extensively presented his view of the purposes of small groups in the church. He noted four ways in which Christian fellowship in small groups helps people:

(1) Fellowship helps the individual to find faith; (2) Fellowship helps people to develop faith; (3) Fellowship helps people to multiply faith; and (4) Fellowship helps people to apply faith.[3]

Writing in *Christ and This Crisis*, Shoemaker spoke of the value of small groups as giving "the encouragement of knowing that other men have the same problems as ours, and if God helps them He can help us too." Such groups, he observed, provide "the firm and friendly challenge of others to the weakness or selfishness of an individual who may unconsciously be failing to live for the good of others."[4]

Another provocative statement from Shoemaker appears in his lecture "The Nurture of Conversion." There he recommended groups that reach beyond the goals of study and work.

> Groups for study or work together are not enough: if there is to be fellowship there must be prayer together, and there must be freedom to speak freely about their experience, their victories and their defeats. Then the victories of one can help all, and the defeats of one can be helped by all. Here perhaps for the first time people will be helped to say what Christ has done for them. They will be drawn out and trained to say it better another time. There will be the tonic of challenge as well as the pleasantness of fellowship.[5]

When the unknown author of the letter to the Hebrews wrote about Christian meetings, he most likely was referring primarily to the early church's worship assemblies. Nevertheless, his words have significance for all Christian gatherings, especially the small mutual-help groups we are discussing. He challenges Christians to use their gatherings as occasions to encourage one another and to urge one another to love and good works: "Let us consider how we may spur one another on toward love and good deeds. Let us not give up meeting together, as some are in the habit of doing, but let us encourage one another and all the more as you see the Day approaching" (Heb. 10:24–25).

Exceptional Opportunities

The practice of the Twelve Steps among people gathered in small groups truly confronts the church with exceptional opportunities. First, it presents us with the opportunity to reach out with the Gospel to many people searching for spiritual help for their troubled lives and who are perhaps more open than others to hearing about the help God has to offer in Jesus.

Second, the practice of the Twelve Steps by persons associated with mutual-help groups gives us the opportunity to review and affirm the importance of the practice of intentional, goal-directed sanctification. Such practice, in turn, urges us to value mutual-help and support among Christians in small groups. In these groups some or all participants may wish to use a Christian formulation of the Twelve Steps. There everyone can certainly expect and celebrate the fulfillment of Jesus' promise, "Where two or three come together in my name, there am I with them" (Matt. 18:20).

---

1. Theodore Tappert, ed. and trans., *The Book of Concord* (Philadelphia: Fortress Press, 1959), 534.

2. *Luther's Small Catechism with Explanation* (St. Louis: Concordia Publishing House, 1986), 22-23.

3. Samuel M. Shoemaker, *How You Can Help Other People* (New York: E. P. Dutton & Co., Inc., 1946), 96-98.

4. Samuel M. Shoemaker, *Christ and This Crisis* (New York: Fleming H. Revell Co., 1943), 94-95.

5. Samuel M. Shoemaker, "The Nurture of Conversion," [c. 1930], 9, Shoemaker Papers, Record Groups 101-4-31, Episcopal Church Archives, Austin Texas.

Conclusion

Today, millions of people are using the Twelve Step Spiritual Program of Recovery, prepared by Bill W. in the late 1930s, to recover from various addictive illnesses.

Because The Twelve Step Program speaks of God in general terms and intends to produce a spiritual awakening in its practitioners, it challenges the church to shape a responsible biblical response to its principles. In turn, the practice of the steps highlights opportunities for the church to consider.

In this study we have discovered biblical resources that make it possible for God's people to respond to the challenge to assess the Twelve Step Program. These resources are the Bible's teachings about the natural knowledge of God, people's inborn ability outwardly to do good works, and God's rule in the secular sphere. Applied to the Twelve Steps, these teachings demonstrate that the steps need not be rejected out of hand. Rather, the teachings of Scripture indicate that the steps can be viewed as God's gift to provide temporal blessings to those who wish to recover from addiction. At the same time, however, Scripture shows us how the steps are to be understood and used by Christians, and others too, in order to avoid serious perils and receive God's greatest good, eternal salvation through faith in Christ.

In addition to discussing the challenge the steps place before the church, we have looked closely at opportunities the steps offer. First, the steps afford us the extraordinary opportunity as followers of Jesus to share the Gospel with people who suffer because of addictions and are actively looking to a Higher Power for spiritual gifts to promote their recovery. They are people God Himself prepares, through the pain and failure of their lives, to hear the good news of His love and forgiveness in Jesus Christ and in the Gospel to find genuine and satisfying answers for all their needs. To be sure, many are anxious to find the God who gives much more than the steps can ever possibly give. They are searching for what Jesus calls "life in all its fullness" (John 10:10 TEV), life with and from God that has eternal dimensions. On our part we have the privilege of sharing with them the faith, hope, and life of love that God gives us in His Son Jesus, who died for our sins and rose again to make us right with God. When we view the unique opportunity before us, Jesus' words to His disciples compel us to action: "Open your eyes and look at the fields! They are ripe for harvest."

The steps offer Christians a second opportunity: to rededicate ourselves to the Christian task of intentional, goal-directed Christian growth and to the formation of mutual-care groups. In these gatherings we can give and receive help to overcome problems and to grow in the Christian faith and life. God will surely bless our mutual care. As St. Paul writes, "Speaking the truth in love, we will in all things grow up into him who is the Head, that is, Christ" (Eph. 4:15).

The Twelve Steps confront the church with challenge and opportunity that God Himself empowers us to meet. St. Paul assures us that God works in us to will and to do according to His good purpose, adding, "My God will meet all your needs according to his glorious riches in Christ Jesus" (Phil. 4:19).